T0171393

SPACE, PLANNING, AND RURALITY

SPACE, PLANNING, AND RURALITY

Uneven Rural Development in Japan

Shu Kitano

TRAFFORD PUBLISHING

Victoria, B.C., Canada

Order this book online at www.trafford.com
or email orders@trafford.com

Most Trafford titles are also available at major online book retailers.

Printed in Victoria, BC, Canada.

ISBN: 978-1-4269-0953-5 (Soft)

*We at Trafford believe that it is the responsibility of us all, as both individuals
and corporations, to make choices that are environmentally and socially sound.
You, in turn, are supporting this responsible conduct each time you purchase a
Trafford book, or make use of our publishing services. To find out how you are
helping, please visit www.trafford.com/responsiblepublishing.html*

*Our mission is to efficiently provide the world's finest, most comprehensive
book publishing service, enabling every author to experience success.
To find out how to publish your book, your way, and have it available
worldwide, visit us online at www.trafford.com*

Trafford rev. 12/08/2009

 www.trafford.com

North America & international
toll-free: 1 888 232 4444 (USA & Canada)
phone: 250 383 6864 ♦ fax: 812 355 4082 ♦ email: info@trafford.com

FOR MY WIFE,

Hiroko Kitano

AND OUR SONS,

Kei Kitano and Hikaru Kitano

CONTENTS

FIGURES AND TABLE

ABBREVIATIONS

CNDP	Comprehensive National Development Plan
GATT	General Agreement on Tariffs and Trade
GHQ	General Headquarters
ISDN	Integrated Services Digital Network
IT	Information Technology
KPSPS	Kanra River Pumped Storage Power Station Scheme
MAFF	Ministry of Agriculture, Forestry and Fisheries of Japan
MITI	Ministry of International Trade and Industry of Japan
MPT	Ministry of Post and Telecommunications of Japan
NGO	Non-governmental Organization
NREA	Natural Resources and Energy Agency (A division of MITI)
NRVPC	Niiharu Rural Village Park Corporation
OECD	Organization for Economic Co-operation and Development
R&D	Research and Development
RII Index	Regional Information Intensification Index
SAC	Sawada Agricultural Cooperative
TEPCO	Tokyo Electric Power Company
T.I.T.	Tokyo Institute of Technology
UFC	Ueno Foresters' Cooperative
UPC	Ueno Promotion Corporation
VYS	Voluntary Youth Social Workers
WTO	World Trade Organization

PREFACE

The objective of this book is to reveal the limitations of the popular rural development practices in Japan (*mura-okoshi/mura-zukuri*) designed to oppose economic and social decline in rural areas of Japan. The premise of the study is that in the practice of local development, planners and communities need to deal with the contradiction between place and space. Another premise is there is an epistemological difference between planners and residents of the communities in perceiving realities and policies of the locality. The contradiction and epistemological difference are the two sides of the same coin. Six localities in Gunma prefecture are selected for an examination of their paths to development or stagnation.

The first three localities have been successful in local economic promotion, resulting in stabilized settlements. Their development strategies include a cooperative-driven agro-food business (Sawada district), an urban-rural exchange program with one of the wealthiest parts of Tokyo (Kawaba village), and a rural village park project (Niiharu village). On the other hand, the three other localities have been unsuccessful, either in maintaining stable settlements and economic bases (Ueno and Kurabuchi villages), or in preserving the landscape and rural environment (Ogo township), regardless of people's efforts and hopes.

The general finding from these six case studies is that only exceptional localities with privileged conditions of location and resources can survive successfully. Their strategies cannot be readily generalized. Based on their experience and additional examinations of economic and spatial trends in Gunma prefecture, the need for an alternative approach to planning should be proposed. Finally, readers may confront another fundamental question: what is the identity of rural areas in the contemporary era?

The original draft of this book is my Ph.D. dissertation submitted to the Department of City and Regional Planning at Cornell University in 2000. Therefore, figures and interview narratives presented in this book are those from the late 1990s. Of course, the social and economic situation surrounding the localities has always been changing until the present. For example, Niiharu, Kurabuchi, and Ogo merged with adjacent bigger municipalities, according to a strong (neo-liberalistic) policy orientation by the central government. Infrastructures including those for internet and telecommunications, as well as for transportation, must have been improved even in the remote communities in the last decade. The global political-economic circumstances have changed more dramatically. The so-called "New Economy" did not last forever. The 9.11 Conspiracy totally changed the political landscape of the world.

Another important change in the decade is a growing awareness for the negative aspects of globalization and neo-liberalism. Although this study considers economic globalization is *a priori*, there have been growing anti-globalism movements world-wide including participants from rural communities. After I had finished this study, I worked on the research of the social movement against globalism and neo-liberalism advocated by the Mexican civil society and indigenous communities. Regardless of my criticism for David Barkin (Chapter 1), presently, I understand there is another important aspect of the contemporary society represented and practiced by ordinary citizens at the grassroots. Therefore, I have always wondered if I should publish this book or not. In the end, I decided to publish it, because I believe some part of the thesis and implications of the book still have a timeless value, as a text that illustrates an important aspect of the universal and fundamental contradiction within rural areas and that depicts some unwritten aspects of the contemporary Japanese society. However, I must acknowledge that the implications presented in this book are conditionally effective and applicable only when we look localities through the above-mentioned premises with the two preconditions: 1) there is the spatial differentiation among localities in vital economic geography; and 2) the localities intend not to accept economic stagnation and decline but economic development or at least vitalization in any forms.

This book could complete with support given by numbers of people. I would like to express my sincere gratitude to my academic advisers for their continuous guidance, unfailing encouragement, and hearty support—given with patience and friendship—throughout the period of my doctoral studies. Professor Thomas Vietorisz was consistently patient and extremely supportive in many ways. I very much appreciate the many insightful comments and suggestions that came with his valuable criticisms, all of which emerged from his deep knowledge of historical materialism and regional planning. Professor William Goldsmith provided much valuable academic input—especially regarding urban and regional theory. I would like to express my appreciation to the Late Professor Arch Dotson, who warmly assisted in the completion of this study. I must also thank my counterparts in Gunma: especially Kazuyuki Yamada (Sawada), Akihiko Miyauchi (Kawaba), Yukio Abe (Niiharu), Yasutoki Asakawa and Yukio Ogawa (Ueno), Kokichi Nakazawa (Kurabuchi), and Masahiro Akutsu (Ogo).

It is my parents, Hirohisa and Hachie Kitano, and my father-in-law, Yakichi Kondo, who have given their constant and unwavering support to my studies.

Finally, my deepest appreciation is given to my wife, Hiroko, and our sons, Kei and Hikaru, who have given the greatest sacrifice throughout the period of my studies. Their steadfast understanding, mental support, and love have always been invaluable source of my inspiration and strength, even in the present.

PART ONE

BACKGROUND

CHAPTER 1
RURAL AREAS IN A GLOBALIZED URBAN WORLD: THE MEANING OF PLACE AND SPACE

"The entire capitalist system...appears as a hierarchical structure of different levels of productivity, and as the outcome of the uneven and combined development of states, regions, branches of industry and firms, unleashed by the quest for surplus profit... Thus *even in the 'ideal case' of a homogenous beginning*, capitalist economic growth, extended reproduction and accumulation of capital are still synonymous with the juxtaposition and constant combination of development and underdevelopment" (Mandel 1975: 102 and 85; quoted in Soja 1989: 94, emphasis added).

1.1. Problem statement

What is sustainable rural development in the age of the global economy? Today, in most advanced industrial societies, rural communities are in crisis. From one point of view—that of traditional core-periphery theory—their unstable situation may be viewed as taking the form of teetering on a knife-blade path: a path between, on one side, progressive depopulation and economic decline and, on the opposite side, unchecked powerful and, in many ways, destructive capitalist development patterns. From another point of view—that of uneven development theory—such a differentiation of rural areas may be seen as part of the more complex uneven process of regional

1

restructuring that is a spatial expression of the profit-maximizing behavior of the capitalist production system (Massey 1984; Markusen 1985). In any case, this geographical dynamism under the capitalist economic system may lead to urban/suburban sprawl, converting ever more remote rural regions, and bringing with it environmental degradation and social problems.[1] This dynamism does, however, not only operate in urban-rural or agriculture-industry relations, but also within world agriculture. Thus, in some regions of the world there is a rapidly growing agro-food industry with highly mechanized farming technologies seeking more efficient means of profit maximization, while in other rural regions, traditional agriculture, as well as traditional rural industry, are losing their primary role as an important basis for the economy. Uneven development of rural regions is a universal issue.

There is a common term, *the global economy* or *globalization*, that describes the present stage of capitalist development. Generally speaking, the first three quarters or, at least, two quarters of the twentieth century were an era of state-driven industrialization accompanying powerful urbanization. These forces affected physical space, people's mentality, and way of life. During this process the ultimate objectives of the state and industrial capitalists were essentially the same. In the present age of the global economy, there is an ever growing dominance of multinational capital in all dimensions of economic activity. Regions and localities, including both cities and villages, are being transformed. Nothing on earth can be isolated from these forces. No one can escape the global economy's influence.

Regardless of this reality, there is a popular term, *sustainable development*, which—since the 1980's and, especially, in the last decade—is frequently spoken of with favor by policy makers and practitioners. In addition, in the last several decades, we have witnessed growing awareness of ecological and environmental concerns within the international community.

For example, David Barkin, a well-known social scientist in rural development, advocates the concept of an autonomous development strategy for sustainable development in rural areas based on his extensive research in Mexican rural communities (Barkin 1998). Rural communities with peasants should, according to Barkin, seek to implement an 'autonomous' production system with ecologically sensitive technologies, including traditional agriculture, ecotourism and related services. His system would also emphasize local food self-sufficiency. I agree with Barkin's affirmation of the need to reverse environmental degradation and to alleviate poverty

---

1 An expression of the "knife-edge path between preservation and destruction" is used in Soja (1989: 108) in reference to David Harvey's argument on uneven geographical landscape.

in rural areas. I also do not deny that there is hope for the possibility of (political) self-development or empowerment (Friedmann 1992) in rural communities. Nevertheless, I pose the following question: Can a community enjoy sustainable economic development in isolation from global economic forces, including technological change?[2] We are, after all, living in a modern capitalist world.

One might pose a second question: Is direct integration with the global economy the only means for community development? The answer to this is, of course, "No." Then, once again, what is a sustainable rural community? Is it possible to build a sound economic base in rural communities while preserving their fundamentally rural environment?

Japan's remarkable success in post-World War II economic development has been extensively documented in various social science fields as the prime example of successful state-guided industrialization for economic growth. The state played an active role in industrial policy through the intervention, regulation, and taming of the market and business communities for economic growth. These measures were accompanied by strong restraints on the maldistribution of wealth. Nevertheless, even this developmental state cannot find a solution to, or escape from, the universal problem of uneven regional and rural development. In this sense, rural Japan is the shadow-side of the so-called development 'miracle.' Upon entering into the latest phase of world capitalism, regional disparity seems to have accelerated. We may anticipate, as well, urban decline and neighborhoods of poverty casting their shadows on the miracle as the Japanese economy expresses geographical unevenness at various levels.

This study is concerned with the development of rural communities in the prefecture of Gunma, on the fringe of Tokyo, the global city, where uneven development is in progress. The study is, therefore, concerned with the alternate side of Japan's development, that is, with a little known aspect of one of the successful developmental states.

This is neither a study of Japan nor a study of agriculture. Instead, I recognize the current rural problem in industrialized societies as a regional problem—not an agrarian or rural problem—and as the

---

2   Some may argue that it is not fair to compare Mexico with advanced industrialized countries, such as Japan. Let me clarify my point: I am not suggesting we can ignore the huge difference in social and economic situations (levels of poverty and availability of income opportunities and basic services, for example) between Mexico and developed countries. My point, however, is that, despite the huge difference, any community, region, or country (both developing and developed) will always be affected by global economic forces, while the outcomes of these forces may be uneven according to a locality's economic, social, political, and geographical conditions.

historical consequence of social, economic, and geographical change under recent global capitalism. The fundamental subject I attempt to explore in this study is alternative planning possibilities for rural areas. These possibilities, must, on the one hand promote rural development, but on the other hand, must, I believe, assume future urban-rural relations that are both desirable for this goal and at the same realistic.

The following chapters and sub-chapters are organized to meet this objective. In the remainder of this chapter, I examine the historical meanings of urban-rural relations and the nature of capitalism with respect to regions, place, and space; this is followed by hypothetical research questions and methodology explanations. In the remainder of Part I, I present a brief historical background of Japanese economic development and examine social and economic trends of Gunma Prefecture, Japan. In Part II, I present case studies of six rural localities in Gunma Prefecture. These localities were chosen as illustrative examples of various scenarios of development, stagnation, and/or underdevelopment. The history and current struggles of the six rural localities are presented and analyzed; extensive use is made of interviews with villagers. Finally, based on the successes and failures of these Gunma villages, in Part III, I discuss the limitations of conventional rural development planning practices. I address the need for a change in the conventional planning mentality as it relates to rural development.

1.2. Theoretical orientation

The need for a historical perspective in order to understand the nature of cities and villages

During any historical period, urban-rural relations are an essential feature of human society, and one of the primary aspects of the historically defined urban-rural relations is the social relations of production.

Although this fundamental point may not be obvious, it is the basic force that shapes the visible social, economic, environmental, and/or political phenomena in rural regions today. Taking an ideological perspective in which 'rural' simply represents 'agrarian' (or agricultural) societies, and 'urban' principally represents 'industrial' societies, is not an appropriate way to look at—and discuss—contemporary rural development problems. In fact, today, as a result of the spread of manufacturing industries to—and improved transportation in—rural areas, rural populations have largely become a wage labor proletariat in non-agricultural employment. Even within the farming sector, a significant portion of farmers in advanced industrialized societies is only part-time. The 1978 OECD Report reports that between 40% and 60% of farmers in member countries are part-time, defined as having more than

50% of household income coming from off-farm jobs (Fuller 1984: 202).[3] In this sense, they are already semi-proletariat (Lobao 1996: 87).

In what follows, I briefly outline approaches to this problem suggested by Max Weber and other late 19th to early 20th century theorists—the Chicago School of Sociology and the New Urban Economics.

Urban-rural relations in Tönnies, Weber, the Chicago School, and the New Urban Theory

Various scholarly traditions have attempted to deal with urban-rural relations in the context of defining city or urban. Generally speaking, one of the most popular and influential concepts for distinguishing the quality of being rural from that of being urban is Tönnies's classic typology using *gemeinschaft* and *geselltschaft* as ideal types (Tönnies 1963). This typology still seems influential and deeply rooted in people's minds. Likewise, Max Weber's classical urban-rural dichotomy distinguishes cities and villages based on such criteria as dominant industrial/occupational types, residential patterns, communal kinship, and political/administrative forms (Weber 1958). In the 1920s, the rural sociologists Sorokin and Zimmerman attempted to build on Weber's distinction by adding new social, economic, environmental, and demographic criteria to their typologies of "Urban World" and "Rural World" (1929: 56-57).[4]

Urban sociologists in the Chicago school tradition developed an influential concept of 'urbanism' in which distinctive urban life styles are essentially assumed to expand to suburbs and rural regions in an unchecked manner (Wirth 1938; Fischer 1984). Their definition of urbanism establishes ideal types of urban/industrial society, and of rural/folk society. They assume an urban-rural continuum in which cities and villages are socio-culturally continuous and their differentiation takes place according to the degree of acceptance of 'urbanism,' i.e., according to their acceptance of "urban" social, human ecological, and social psychological characteristics (Takahashi 1988: 300).[5] However, the Chicago School's arguments on urbanism lack a serious consideration of the social relations of production as an essential dynamic of the capitalist society. Because of its insufficiently scientific definition of 'urban,' Castells (1976) regards the Chicago School's arguments merely as 'urban ideology.'

---

3 In Japan, it was 79% in 1990, if this definition is adopted.
4 See Sorokin and Zimmerman (1929), for example.
5 For a comprehensive review of classical and recent debates on the urban-rural continuum, see Pahl (1996).

New Urban Economic theorists, including geographers and urban sociologists, support the view that cities and villages are economically and spatially continuous with respect to capital accumulation and its spatial (or geographical) appearance, but they also differ in critical ways from the Chicago School. According to the New Urban Economic Theory, under the capitalist mode of production, ever sprawling urbanization, accompanied by geographical accumulation of capital, and uneven development of space are driven by the dynamics of capital. Harvey (1985: 127-128) views "urban" as a continuous basin system with a core and peripheries. He argues that the distinction between urban and rural is now meaningless with respect to production functions; the distinction between rural is, rather, an expression of the spatial division of consumption. In this sense, regardless of their visible physical landscape, rural villages are no longer 'rural' in the traditional sense. The extent of the relationship of rural to the economic core (cities and urban areas) is the critical element. The relationship (given through transportation, technology, and location) determines for rural areas the availability of multiple economic bases and business opportunities.

Early post World War II rural sociologists tended to adopt a relatively narrower view of urban-rural relations, viewing them from the farmer's (or agrarian) perspective as in a sociology of agriculture (Lobao 1996: 83-84). For them the rural/agrarian dependency on cities/industries was a central area of concern. However, the New Urban Theory has evolved in ways which, I believe, make it applicable to the contemporary rural development issues with which policy makers and planners must deal, namely, limitless urban sprawl and peripheral rural decline. In fact, this is not a 'rural problem' but a 'regional problem.'[6]

To consider contemporary social, economic, and environmental problems in any region, an understanding of production relations over space, including those between city and village is important. For this Marxist political economics provides a useful theoretical foundation and analytical perspective.

Living with the contradiction: Rural community as "place" and as "space"

One cannot deny the uniqueness of a rural place and people's life there as distinctively different from that of an urban place. People often tend to link such distinctiveness of rural life and environment with ecological/cultural ideologies based on a site-specific, place-bound perception. Nevertheless, I

---

6   For the detailed debates between the Chicago school's and Marxian urban sociologists, refer to Comparative Urban Research, vol. VI, No. 2 and 3, 1978, including Harvey (1978), Fischer (1978), and Bensman (1978), for example.

propose that there must be another way to look at contemporary rural or, more accurately, regional problems in advanced industrialized societies. Marxist urban theory suggests that cities and villages are continuous entities, driven to this continuity by the universal social, economic, and spatial dynamics of a world-historical process of the capitalist mode. This process takes place regardless of visible differences in demography, cultural values, physical landscapes, and dominant economic activities. The underlying concept here is 'space,' not place.

We must understand that everyone in a region, locality, or community is affected by the past and by the present, and that there is a dualistic nature of any locality—'place' as a particularistic concept and 'space' as a relative one (Lobao 1996:77).

(1) *Place* is an empirical concept that reflects local identity or *genius loci*. In rural areas "place" has its origin as "a fragment of agro-pastoral space" (Lefebvre 1991: 234). "Place" is a subjective vernacular entity expressing people's experience and a locality's history. Every locality has its own identity as a *place*, an identity that has been nourished by a unique historical context including natural environment, architecture, topography, physical distance from the outside, cultural (often religious) values, and tribal/communal customs. It is appropriate to quote Relph (1993: 34), because his explanation seems to be closest to the image of *place* , as I define it in this section:

"A place is a whole phenomenon, consisting of the three intertwined elements of a specific landscape with both built and natural elements, a pattern of social activities that should be adapted to the advantages or virtues of a particular location, and a set of personal and shared meanings."

One often possesses an intimate feeling of nostalgia with respect to his or her *place*. In Japanese, the term, *furusato*, meaning "a native place" with the connotation of a countryside or rural village, is frequently used when people speak of rural areas. The value of rural areas as part of a country's cultural heritage is often spoken of in this context. Thus, people often consider place and absolute space as being identical. Consider, for example, Gottfried's explanation of rural landscape:

"People's intense experiences with the land have enhanced the cultural value of rural areas. Most rural landscapes are "constructed"—that is, they show a many-layered history of human intervention. Cultural conservation holds an important place in rural policy because it reinforces the sensory experience of the rural landscape and strengthens landscape's role as a symbol of stability" (1995: 13).

Yet places are not merely remnants of the past, but rather their "local identities," as cultural expressions of the outside world, are changing. In this sense, place can mean 'bounded performance' at a particular historical moment (Harvey 1996: 294). In the context of *place*, the urban-rural dichotomy proposed by earlier sociologists is still a useful concept and effective language for taking into account differences in social and physical elements between urban and rural regions. Nevertheless, while it is common for people to view *place* in a parochial way—as a (culturally, socially, or sometimes economically) bounded territory (Massey 1993: 143), there is another dimension of place in the broader context of political economy to which social scientists must pay serious attention.

(2) *Space* is both an abstract and an objective concept for describing society (Castells 1992). The concept of space has been developed in the tradition of western Marxist theorists based on the work of Lefebvre (Soja 1989: 43-51).[7] Unlike place, *space* (as *espace abstrait* or abstract space in Lefebvre's term) is a continuous entity—not a bounded territory. *Space* is best recognized as a contradiction of capital accumulation as capitalism evolves. Capital does not belong to any *place*; rather it is highly mobile spatially. Uneven regional development is an inevitable consequence of uneven capital accumulation, accompanying socio-spatial differentiation between a core and peripheries and/or a spatial division of labor. Castells (1977: 115) gives an explicit definition of *space*:

"Space is a material product, in relation with other material elements—among others, men, who themselves enter into particular social relations, which give to space (and to the other elements of the combination) a form, a function, a social signification. It is not, therefore, a mere occasion for the deployment of the social structure, but a concrete expression of each historical ensemble in which a society is specified."

Lobao (1996: 88) provides a summary of the nature of *space*:

"Global economic change is an uneven process over time and within and between nations. It transforms economic structure. It alters social relations or class structure and other asymmetrical power relations of gender, age, and ethnicity, brings about new strategies of state intervention, and affects the levels at which populations are able to reproduce themselves. As a consequence, places are differentiated with regard to production structures, social relations, demographic and other characteristics reflective of local reproduction, ..."

---

7   Refer to Lefebvre (1991), for example.

Hence, Harvey argues that 'urban' is the agglomeration of physical infrastructure and facilities for production, exchange, and consumption as a necessary means of capital accumulation for reproduction (using his term, 'urban built environment'), which is one material aspect of space and is the appropriation of space (1985: 1994). In this sense, what we call rural areas (except those rural areas where resource-exploitative, mechanistic, industrial agriculture is operated) in terms of landscape are increasingly a spatial periphery of the global capitalist system. Hence, a rural space does not imply a stationary state; instead rural space changes constantly in relation to the whole social-economic process that always takes place unevenly.

In primitive pre-capitalist societies, there was no (or little) difference between place and space. Their differentiation is the product of history. In the early capitalist mode of production, then-existing semi-autonomous rural (or agrarian) communities were forced to be involved in the process of exchange for goods and services produced in the cities (a *spatial* practice). Nevertheless their local identity as 'rural' in a cultural or socio-ecological sense tended to remain the same (a *place* practice). Unlike manufacturing and service industries, agriculture is a space-based activity, applying labor to a specific place and using extensive physical space for its production. Therefore peripheral spaces where urban agglomeration does not occur could be said, in theory, to be specialized in farming. (Mizuoka 1992: 234). Yet this perception would no longer be correct under the current GATT/WTO international trade regime that advocates a global economy.

Under the current regime, food production can shift internationally, for example from domestic locations (with labor-intensive agricultural operations which are economically inefficient) to other locations where intensive capital investment is possible (the midwestern United States, for example), or where cheap farm labor is available (rural areas in the third world and, to some extent, areas in the United States that employ low-wage migrant labor).

In contemporary society, we are living in a dualistic spatial environment in which there are always communications, negotiations, and conflicts between a *place* and a *space*. In this world, the visible physical landscape of a locality can be understood as a product of the interaction between *place*, as an expression of local identity, and *space*, which is the product of a broader regional, national, and global political and economic system. While there may be a tendency to view all rural areas, i.e., those looking "rural," as *place*, those rural areas dominated by capital-intensive industrial agriculture and related agro-industry (both of which form a kind of quasi-urban built environment) must be regarded as fundamentally *different* spaces.

1.3. Environmental concerns and rural place/space

Regardless of the spatial nature of rural areas, they still retain the physical and biological uniqueness of rural areas. This uniqueness increases the social value of rural areas, as Marsden and Murdoch (1991) maintain: [d]espite its absolute and relative decline, in terms of traditional economic relations, agriculture continues to dominate rural land-use and property rights, and represents cultural and environmental authenticity in rural life in policy and popular discourses.[8] This perception supports popular arguments, based on ecological and environmental perspectives, for a reconsideration of the social function of agriculture and rural space in industrialized countries.

In environmental, ecological, and/or communitarian arguments, the following are key issue areas:

(1) *Environment, ecology, and health*: These include ecological preservation, the reduction of the environmental burden caused by intensive agricultural production activities, and a growing awareness of food safety and the benefits of organic farm production;

(2) *Natural resource and disaster management*: This relates to the need for stewardship. Through certain types of farming and forestry production activities, people in rural areas, especially farmers and foresters, could serve as stewards of the land, water, and forests;[9] and

(3) *Social amenity (including welfare and education)*: This relates to rural areas as providers of social amenities, as places for recreation and rest, and places for extra-curricular education and for the cultivation of aesthetic sensitivity.[10]

---

8 Quoted in Whatmore (1994: 55).

9 Agenda 21 (adopted at the 1992 UNCED meeting in Rio de Janeiro) emphasizes that "mountains are a particularly fragile environment, and recommends that close attention should be paid to both ecological and social questions," and it maintains that "programme areas cover strengthening knowledge about ecology and sustainable development of mountain ecosystems and promoting integrated watershed development and alternative livelihood opportunities" (Osti 1997: 181). In Japan this could probably be interpreted as a need for maintaining mountainous rural communities, which undertake natural resource management and land preservation in agro-geographically handicapped areas. As a result of narrow and mountainous topography and heavy precipitation, rice paddies in these regions have long been functioning as semi-natural dams during the rainy season, and, thus, may have prevented massive floods and soil erosion.

10 It is remarkable that, according to an opinion poll taken by the Japanese Prime Minister's Office, Japanese urban dwellers show a great appreciation for—and awareness of—the amenities of rural areas: for example, people chose the following two as the most significant social functions of rural areas: "places for recreation/rest" (59.1%); and "places where our cultural traditions are preserved" (38.9%).

These three issue areas include a wide array of contemporary environmental issues, such as toxic and chemical regulation, water and air quality control, and historic preservation—of both physical space and cultural heritage. I expect that, aside from the ideology and romanticism of arguments of this sort,[11] they do raise valid concerns about quality of life issues, and, therefore, these non-economic functions of rural place, as represented in the ecological/environmental arguments, need to be maintained for the optimal benefit to society. Various aspects of these concerns are demonstrated, both ideologically and practically, in the local politics of the case studies presented later.

Nevertheless, I must point out that these arguments tend to view environmental issues only as place-particular, or embedded subjects, and largely ignore their meaning from the standpoint of place/space duality. These issues must also be seen as the past and present manifestation of place/space contradictions and the globalizing capitalist mode of production. We must consider:

"the material and institutional issues of how to organize production and distribution in general, how to confront the realities of global power politics and how to displace the hegemonic powers of capitalism not simply with dispersed, autonomous, localized, and essentially communitarian solutions" (Harvey 1996: 400).

I do not propose a drastic political project against capitalism; however, I do suggest that we have to be sensitive to the space in which production, consumption, distribution, and accumulation are taking place. My dialectic proposition is that a realistic alternative solution will be identified only when we control, transform, or, at least, tame the negative aspects of the current mode of production, which is the essential force in generating environmental and ecological issues.

In the meantime, I agree with the view that now, as in the future, we still need 'rural' in some way. The question is, in what way? *That* is the central question of this book.

1.4. Central research questions

My essential position is that we need to maintain rural communities and environments, even in a highly modern industrialized/urbanized society. The central research questions to be explored through critical examination of local development and planning practices in selected rural localities are: (1) What implications can we draw from my research for alternative policies

---

11 See Harvey (1996, especially Part II) for a comprehensive critique of popular ecological-environmental discourse from the standpoint of historical materialism.

and planning strategies that can guide us in appropriate directions for rural and regional development?; and (2) How can planners deal with the regional contradictions of this capitalist society?

From the above historical and theoretical perspective I put forth the following three propositions:

(1) Unevenness of rural development and regional differentiation may be found not only between different regions with different historical and geographical backgrounds, but also within a relatively compact territorial unit in which local communities once shared relatively similar social origins and homogeneous economic and industrial structures.

(2) The urban-rural relationship is always a critical aspect of regional development. Taking into account the socio-spatial nature of the current mode of production, there is reason for skepticism about the beautifully-harmonized ecologically-symbiotic relationship between cities and the rural countryside, referred to as sustainable rural development. There is another reality that planners must be aware of, namely that sustainable development is incompatible with the market fundamentalism that characterizes our globalizing capitalist system (Soros 1998: xxi-xxiii).

(3) Planners currently have limited power to propose policies for dealing with regional problems as contradictions within capitalism.

To the extent that these propositions can be supported, they should serve as a guide for the political mobilization of public opinion aimed at a reconsideration of the future roles of rural communities. In order to investigate these propositions, I established the following areas of inquiry for my case studies:

(1) The identification of conditions that make possible the exceptional performance of so-called successful local development or revitalization, including locational factors, resource availability, institutional strengths/weaknesses. What are the localities' strengths and weaknesses? What factors can contribute to work in favor of these development strategies, and which will not?

(2) An inquiry into existing or possible communication modes that make preserving local (rural) identities within a sustainable development strategy possible: Are the selected rural localities able to communicate with higher-order cultures and economies? If yes, in what way? If no, why not, and what could be done about it?

(3) An identification of the gap (if it exists) between local policy makers/planners' perceptions and explanations and those of other citizens? How and why do they perceive the changing geography differently? This is a question considered from an epistemological perspective.

(4) A reconsideration of the meaning of popular local development strategies in Japan (*mura-okoshi*): What are their implications (both negative and positive)? What can we learn from them?

Regardless of the earlier discussion, the class relations within a village or between cities and villages will be given little direct attention in this study. Rather, I treat them as essential premises underlying all social and economic phenomena within regions.[12]

1.5. Methods of inquiry

I employ a planning methodology that is firmly established in the U.S. but unusual for a political-economic study in Japan. The main data base for this study is a broad set of field interviews. One of the reasons I use this methodology is my past experience as a planning official for rural and agricultural development in the Ministry of Agriculture, Forestry and Fisheries (MAFF) of Japan. It was there that I developed skepticism about the sources of information that were used (official information and statistical data sent from lower administrative authorities). I felt that there was a gap between the local people and me as a policy analyst.

Therefore, for this study, I decided to conduct my research and to do a qualitative analysis based on local citizens' views. I believe that ordinary citizens are largely ignorant of planning theory, and that their perceptions are largely dominated by a sense of *place*—with no awareness of *space*. Their explanations are likely to be misconceptions about reality; in addition, they are normally poorly informed about the economics and politics of the outside world. Nevertheless, I believe that the true voices of those living and working with—and struggling against—the regional contradictions represent an indispensable information source. Their voices need to be analyzed with a sound theoretical background. They could also undoubtedly serve as a valuable means for describing the changing world. I treat interview narratives (combined with my responses and critical examinations) as my primary source material for discussion and analysis.

For nine months, from May to July 1998, and from February to July 1999, I interviewed more than 150 people (24 - 34 interviewees per case study) in six rural localities in Gunma. There were two categories of interviewees:

(1) Those involved with local policy as professionals, including planning officials at village/township offices, assemblymen, a mayor, and professional consultants, including professors; and (2) ordinary people, including farmers, local businessmen, shop owners, housewives, students, company/factory

---

12 I agree with Hoggart and Buller (1987) who reject as myth the popular view of agrarianism that a rural locality is a class-free society.

workers, and high school teachers. The second category included men and women, old and young. In selecting individuals for interviews, I had to rely primarily on my local counterparts in village/township offices or other local authorities. In addition, some 'rush' interviews were undertaken without formal appointments. To avoid biased representation and to assure diversity, I asked my counterparts to adhere to the following selection principles with respect to potential interviewees:

(1) There must be one or two interviewees from every occupational, age, and gender category listed (Appendix A).

(2) Interviewees were not to be selected from a single, or from a few, residential communities (hamlets); instead they were to be selected to assure, insofar as was possible, a fair representation with respect to residential districts within a village/township.

(3) Interviewees must not be selected from a single political orientation; the list must include those both pro- and anti- mayor and local government.

With respect to (1) and (2), fairly acceptable sampling was achieved. This is a necessary condition for a social scientific inquiry. As for (3), although I have no means to confirm, through formal analysis, that this condition was satisfied, nevertheless, both positive and negative comments on current policy and performance demonstrate that a variety of view points was represented.

Interviews were guided by pre-designed interview sheets. Two different interview sheets were prepared for the two categories of respondents (Appendix B). In most cases, interviews were followed by an open-ended, in-depth interview on such topics as daily life and the future of the community. Average interview times were approximately 40 - 60 minutes.

In addition, document research was undertaken for the purpose of correcting provisional background information about each village/township, including historical settings, social, economic, and demographic trends, and for outlining both current and past local programs. The main sources for these data are official statistics and reports published by various local organizations, including village/township offices, agricultural cooperatives, chambers of commerce, the prefectural government of Gunma, and universities.

CHAPTER 2
THE CONTEXT OF JAPANESE
NATIONAL DEVELOPMENT

"The city came to be seen not only in its distinctive role as a centre for industrial production and accumulation, but also as the control point for the reproduction of capitalist society in terms of labour power, exchange, and consumption patterns. .....The older agrarian peripheries were either partially urbanized or left relatively alone, but their key role in supplying cheap labour, food, raw materials, and markets was increasingly transposed to the 'external' colonies" (Soja 1989: 95 and 166).[13]

The purpose of this chapter is to provide some historical background material on rural/regional development in Japan as a backdrop for the case studies in later chapters. I will do this from two different angles. First, I will present a brief history of regional (spatial) differentiation as a consequence of capitalist development and national policies. Second, I will provide a background for contemporary rural development policies in Japan—often called *mura-okoshi* (translated as village promotion or vitalization). One may see some sort of causation between national development policies (for the making of a "growth machine") and local response to this, which is often carried out by local policy makers and elites, in many rural areas. This presentation will give readers an understanding of why an agro-centric, communitarian mentality has been

---

13 Here, Soja primarily refers to the international division of labor that resulted from imperialist practices of the early industrialized countries. Nevertheless, one might see a similar picture in the changing rural-urban relations in Japan during the period of post-World War II economic (capitalist) development.

nourished among practitioners of rural development in Japan. However, at the end of the chapter, I critique this approach, a critique which is developed in the remaining chapters.

2.1. Economic development and regional change

Historical background

Japan experienced its industrial revolution in the 1890s, just after the Meiji Restoration (1868). The combination of the Meiji Restoration and the industrial revolution altered the nation's political economic system from feudalism to capitalism. The characteristics of Japanese capitalism can be summarized in the following two paragraphs (Hasumi 1968: 21):

(1) Since Japanese capitalism developed much later than capitalism did in western nations, Japan could employ western manufacturing technologies and machinery, most of which were already developed during the European Industrial Revolution period. Thus, there was an insufficient demand for labor to promote the differentiation of the peasantry; and

(2) Commodity production during the period of pre-capitalist eras still predominantly operated inside rural villages, and it was never developed to a satisfactory level to be transferred to urban manufacturing. Also, unlike European agriculture, being rice paddy-based, Japanese agriculture was, at that time, unable to improve production by introducing crop rotation. Thus, enclosure never occurred in Japan.

These factors had a significant effect on the character of Japanese rural societies: rural areas retained their subsistence farmers and some aspects of the traditional Asiatic mode of production characteristics of pre-modern Japan for a long time, even after World War II (Ouchi 1963: 127-133). As part of democratization policies of the GHQ (General Headquarters of the occupation force), compulsory land reform was enacted during 1947-50, in order to do away with traditional landlord-peasant relations.[14] It was only after land reform that rural areas in Japan abandoned their "Asiatic" structure. Thus, Japan's post-World War II economic development provides a good example of rapid social-economic change under industrialized capitalism.

As part of the pre World War I industrial revolution, the imperial government promoted light industries, including textiles for export, as well as the iron industry. But until World War II, about half of the Japanese population remained agrarian—the vast majority poor peasants—tenants and

---

14 This reform gave Japanese agriculture a unique, but critical, characteristic—that is, extreme "smallness" in the scale of farming, which, although it created millions of owner cultivators, also created a lack of competitiveness in the world agricultural market.

small holders. Today the farming population represents less than 5% of the total. As for land ownership, traditional landlords still functioning in ways reminiscent of the Asiatic mode of production remained dominant until land reform in the 1940s, despite the industrial revolution of the 1890s.

It is of interest for this thesis that the first state-owned silk-spinning mill in Japan was established in Tomioka, Gunma Prefecture in 1873 with the latest machines and technology imported from France. It was later privatized. As a result, until after World War II, Gunma villages enjoyed prosperity based on sericulture for the silk industry.

Post-World War II industrialization and employment change: Phase 1

Post-World War II economic policies emphasized heavy industry and chemicals and later high-tech industries. Inputs for these industries were imported. This contributed dramatically to the attainment of a strategic intent—"Match the standard of living of the West" (Vietorisz and McAdams 1995: 7), with the guidance of expert state bureaucrats.

Post World War II industrialization can be divided into two phases. In 1955 Japan entered the first phase of its hyper- growth period. During the early years of this phase, the industrial structure was shifted under the government's industrial policy from traditional light industries, such as textiles, to modern heavy industries, such as mechanical and metal industries. This changes created a large demand for capital investment by big corporations, which greatly contributed to economic growth. At the same time, a great demand for industrial labor was created. Since the dual structure of the pre-World War II Japanese economy was characterized by Asiatic stagnation,[15] There was significant "disguised unemployment" of the rural population (in other words, latent surplus population), and this permitted a large shift of labor from agriculture to industry. During the decade of 1955-65, 60% of the newly created industrial labor demands was filled by an agrarian population. One of the important points about this huge labor shift is that 70% of these rural migrants were younger than 19, their youth made it possible for them to adjust easily to the rapidly evolving technological improvements taking place throughout Japanese industry. Nevertheless, this labor shift never created a situation that could be characterized as "over-migration" (Vietorisz and McAdams 1995: 10), due to the fact that there was simultaneously a satisfactory increase in agricultural productivity and to the later introduction

---

15 A society in Asiatic stagnation is typically characterized by the following two conditions: "the perpetuation of the ancient systems of communal land ownership" and "the ambiguous social division of labor that leaves the village community completely unaltered" (Tökei 1979: 16).

17

of regional industrialization. As a result, the farm population (including farm workers and their dependents) decreased dramatically. For example, during the period 1955-80, it decreased by 53%.

Industrial decentralization: Phase 2 of hyper growth

In the early years of post-World War II industrialization, significant labor migration took place from villages to what were then major industrial-metropolitan regions, such as Tokyo/Kawasaki/Yokohama, Osaka/Kobe, Nagoya, and Fukuoka/Kita-Kyushu. But starting in the 1960s, industrial decentralization was planned and implemented under the First Comprehensive National Development Plan (CNDP or *Zenkoku sogokaihatsu keikaku*) of 1962. Under this plan a number of branch plants and subcontractors were created as the lowest part of the hierarchy of the Japanese industrial system at that time. Decentralization meant the transplantation of branch plants to—and the creation of subcontractors in—more remote regions, while the core business functions largely remained in Tokyo and/or to a lesser extent in Osaka. This marked the second phase of rapid economic growth,[16] during which more emphasis was placed on developing export-oriented manufactures, such as automobiles and electronics, in the form of *keiretsu*. Farmer workers (industrial wage earners who were, at the same time, part-time farmers) gradually became more prominent due to expanding regional and rural industrialization.[17] Today, 85% of farm households are part-time farmers.

Some argue that this rural economic structure, with a dominance of part-time farmers, allows capitalists to obtain relatively cheap labor for the lower end of their *Keiretsu* structure. Since productivity increases in the industrial sector are more rapid than those in the agricultural sector, the income gap between industry and agriculture has gradually expanded, and, hence, part-time farmers have naturally come to rely on non-farm income more and more.

In sum, the second phase of post-World War II growth was characterized by decentralization, which promoted the integration of rural space into newly developed urban/industrial cores under a hierarchical industrial structure.

Stable growth after the 1970s and the Bubble Economy in the 1980s

Since the oil crises of the 1970s, the base of the Japanese economy has shifted away from heavy industry and chemicals and toward greater reliance on the high-tech electronic and automobile industries, as well as the service industry,

---

16 Generally 1961 to 1965 or the early 1970s.
17 For example, implementation of the New Industrial-City Promotion Act of 1962, and the Special Industrial Area Promotion Act of 1964.

marking the beginning of a slower growth period. The most characteristic change in industrial space during this time was agglomeration of offices, business functions, and ultimately capital in the Tokyo region, along with the relative decline of other business/industrial cores—most typically in the Osaka and Kansai regions including Kobe and Kyoto (Miyamoto 1993; Hill and Fujita 1995). In other words, this period was marked by the emergence of Tokyo as a global city. Core business functions, such as headquarters and R&D of these new industrial sectors, located in and around the greater Tokyo area, while traditional heavy industrial districts established during the 1950s and 1960s declined.

Another characteristic feature of this period is that the farm crisis became more tangible, partly because of the reduced profitability of domestic small-scale agriculture and of repeated market liberalization of agricultural commodities and primary products. As a result, rural spatial differentiation, including peripheral decline of rural areas and urban/suburban integration, became more visible. In many peripheral regions, the natural decrease of population, which ultimately leads to community extinction, has become larger and more visible due to a loss of younger reproductive populations.

The reasons that rural people still migrate to cities are attributable not only to the farm crisis and a lack of non-farm jobs in rural areas, but also to poor public services and education. In Japan, although public education— elementary and secondary (junior high)—is mandatory and universally provided, there are still gaps between cities and villages in terms of facilities and quality of teaching. Admission to top universities (most of which are located in Tokyo, Osaka, and Kyoto) is based on performance in a competitive admissions exam. Generally, good senior high schools are located in/around big cities. Normally, senior high school age students from more remote rural regions, if they chose to attend these superior schools, would have to reside in dormitories or apartments and live separately from their parents, so that the parents would pay extra costs for their children's education. In addition, attending a private night or week-end preparatory school for success in college admissions exams is common among high school students. These services are not available in villages. This problem will be demonstrated in the chapter on Ueno village.

In the late 1980s, the so-called Bubble Economy, with sky-rocketing speculative real-estate prices, hit entire areas of Japan's islands, particularly those of big cities, and to some extent, the rural regions. "Unplanned chaotic nature of Japanese urbanization" has been remarkable elsewhere in Japan (Castells 1998: 229), along with the boom of housing development in urban suburbs and resort development (ski areas, golf courses, theme parks, and so forth) in rural regions.

Then, finally, in the mid 1990s, a long winter came to the Japanese economy.

A new phase of the capitalist mode: The global information economy

With technological innovation, especially of electronic tele-communication networks, we are entering the age of the information society. Technological innovations, especially those in communication and transportation, dramatically reduce the cost of 'distance.' They enhance the spatial mobility of corporate capital. Conventional manufacturing industry has moved to areas where less expensive, but relatively skilled, labor is available in search of maximized profit, while the industrial structure of advanced economies has shifted to one that is more service-based and more knowledge/information-based.

The age of the global information economy is the latest phase of world capitalist development. Its essential dynamic may ultimately lead to the transformation of social relations of production in the capitalist system. Vietorisz argues that Marx "already perceives...what is central to the emerging information era of our day: that the creation of real social wealth grows out of proportion with labor input...and comes to depend primarily on science and technology. ...With this historical change, value, as the measure of labor time and the focus of production relations, becomes inappropriate and... dysfunctional." Thus paradoxically, market value, even as it dominates our rapidly globalizing capitalist information economy, "reaches its limits and burns itself out" (1991: 17-18). Information itself, though it is made into a commodity and has a market price, cannot be regarded on a par with traditional mass-produced commodities. The ground has shifted under the 19th-20th Century production system.

This can be a double-edged sword for regional development. On the one hand, it has the potential to release regions (including rural regions) from conventional location and geographical constraints. On the other hand, if investments in this context are allowed to take place in a *laissez faire* manner, they will be concentrated mostly in urban and metropolitan regions. This would make permanent the spatial disparity of production and accumulation, and, as a result, could cause a lasting economic and geographical marginalization of certain rural areas. While metropolitan regions would enjoy producing information as their highest productivity activity, some rural areas would be forced to give up the production of even conventional goods and services, including the production of raw materials and manufacturing inputs.

Castells, who has done extensive empirical research on Japanese society and public policy, considers the Japanese model of a developmental state no longer effective in the global information society, and he warns of the need to transform many aspects of the social, economic, and political systems and institutions (1998: 214-28).

Undoubtedly the changes accompanying the new information society will affect rural areas, both as space and place. And they may or may not strengthen further the trend toward uneven rural and regional development and spatial differentiation. Under these circumstances, all communities, both urban and rural, will be required to do something for their survival, preservation, and transformation.

2.2. Popular movements for local (self-) development

I believe that uneven rural and regional development is an expression of the contradiction of a modern capitalist society. In the Japanese context, it could also be interpreted as the contradiction of regional planning in Japan. From the point of view of a developmental state, regional planning means the design and implementation of an allocation policy for the purpose of making a growth machine.

It was after the 1980s that the popular word, *mura-okoshi* (translated "village revitalization"), referring to a kind of self-development initiative utilizing unique local resources and knowledge, came into common usage. *Mura-okoshi* has been recognized as a movement in rural Japan. It is both a practice and an ideology. Local-based or so-called endogenous rural revitalizing efforts are usually regarded as essential to *mura-okoshi*.

Traditional bases for modern self-development movements

Although significantly different from contemporary *mura-okoshi*, there is a tradition of *mura-okoshi*-like local development practices in Japan. Examples of roots of contemporary *mura-okoshi* can be found in rural development efforts in the pre-World War II modernization time.

First, during the mid-*Meiji* era (the 1890s), Maeda initiated the *son-ze* movement,[18] which promoted local social and economic development based upon local-native technologies, capital, and resources. The *son-ze* movement was a response to policies of the *Meiji* Imperial government, which, at that time, was trying urgently to transform the state from a pre-capitalist one into a so-called modern industrial nation. It did this by actively introducing modern Western industrial technologies and political and economic institutions. In the minds of policy makers at that time, there was a strong sense that everything native Japanese was out-of-date, irrelevant, and in need

---

18 Son-ze can be translated as "village rules." Essentially the movement encouraged villagers to establish their own rules or policies for local self-development with local knowledge and resources.

of alteration, including, among other things, religion, architecture, clothing, and methods of production. "Westernization" was regarded as the ultimate way of "modernization."

Second, during the massive world-wide economic depression in the 1930s, rural Japan—especially northern Japan, such as the Hokkaido (the north island) and Tohoku (North-eastern part of the Main island) regions—suffered a severe economic and social crisis, due to decreased agricultural commodity prices and a record lean harvest during those years.[19] To deal with this situation, the centrally planned *Noson-Keizai-Kosei* (rural economy recovery) Program[20] attempted to promote local industry and agriculture (although it was actually implemented as a political tool for organizing people for the fascist nation and World War II) (Miyamoto 1990: 210).

This history suggests that rural self-development movements in Japan emerge when rural areas and agriculture face a critical situation due to contradictions caused by the domestic and/or international economy.

The legacy of "localism" in the 1970s

Generally speaking contemporary *mura-okoshi* has been defined in terms of the rise of "*chiiki-shugi*" (regionalism or localism) that coincided with the oil crisis of the 1970s. The concept was originally described by a political economist, Tamanoi, in the 1970s. In Tamanoi's regionalism, a region must seek its own economic, political, and cultural identity. This is in contrast with the approach of conventional policy makers who considered a region as belonging to the "center." In Tamanoi's words: "Regionalism could be defined as the efforts that residents in a region seek in order to gain political and economic self-reliance and cultural independence, based on their *fudo* (*genus loci*) with a feeling of solidarity with their community" (quoted in Miyamoto 1990: 210, translated by the author). By the 1980s, however, the voice of regionalism had become weaker, due to shrinking or stagnating public expenditures for regional and rural development that resulted from a worsened national budget and financial situation (Moritomo 1991: 23-24).

Regionalism may be regarded as a reaction against the urban/industry-biased and centralized planning mentality of the developmental state. It triggers awareness of, and sympathy for, local-based action for local self-reliance among both the general public and practitioners, planners, and certain political communities. But I will argue that this form of regionalism

---

19 It is reported that more than 40,000 rural girls were sold for cheap industrial labor due to a severe decline in rural household income during the period of economic crisis.

20 The plan encouraged local-based economic activities, including agricultural processing and other, non-agricultural, family-based industry, such as handicrafts.

does not represent a practical way to alter the trend toward uneven rural and regional development under global capitalism.

The "One-Village-One-Product" movement in the 1980s

The most representative model of contemporary *mura-okoshi* practices is the One-Village-One-Product Movement (*Isson-Ippin* Movement) in Ohita Prefecture on Kyushu Island (a south-western island). This movement began with strong leadership from Governor Morihiro Hiramatsu, a former MITI (Ministry of International Trade and Industry) official, who took office in 1979. His idea was developed out of grass roots actions in rural municipalities of the prefecture (Goto 1993: 10).[21]

The basic idea of this movement is that each municipality in Ohita should have one (preferably high value-added) agricultural product (for example, kiwi fruits of Kunisaki township; Japanese mushrooms of Ohta village; shrimps of Himeshima village), which would be competitive in the national market (Miyamoto 1990: 334-335). The production and processing of this commodity would form the basis of a local-based strategy for development.

"They are the innovation of combining primary products with local processing industries, the emphasis on cooperative efforts between public and private sectors, the emphasis on human resource development, the role of prefectural government as facilitator rather than as primary promoter of development..." (Kiyonari 1986, quoted in and translated by Goto 1993: 12).

However, as Ohita's effort became famous and regarded as a model case, similar practices were introduced nation-wide with the support of policy makers and corporations. As this happened, the practice became politicized and there was diminished emphasis on local socio-economic development. In theory, when this practice spreads nation-wide, there will be a number of municipalities that must compete in the national market for a particular product. Excessive reliance on a single product may be a high risk development strategy for backward rural economies, just as it is for any corporation (Miyamoto 1989: 298).

What is contemporary "mura-okoshi"?

Today, the term *mura-okoshi* is recognized as a general term referring to certain local (rural) development actions or movements. The term is not free from ambiguity.

---

21 For a description of the movement in English, refer to Goto (1993, pp.10-13) and Fujimoto (1992).

It is neither an official nor an academic term. There is no firm definition of it. We can list five characteristics of *mura-okoshi*:[22] (1) an attempt to counteract urban and industrial dominance over regional development; (2) utilization of local resources; (3) emphasis on a self-reliant way of development; (4) bottom-up and territorial approaches to development; and (5) exchange of ideas with other localities (Goto 1993: 7-8). As Goto mentions, the meaning of *mura-okoshi* can "vary from place to place." In examples of so-called *mura-okoshi* policies, we can observe a variety of practices, including local economic development (through agricultural promotion; small-industrial development, such as food processing; rural tourism, and, more recently, urban-rural "exchanges"); environmental preservation; and a search for improved welfare-related services, including health and education. In addition, a territorial unit over which *mura-okoshi* is applied can vary from a small, neighborhood community to an entire prefecture. Goto (1993: 7) maintains *mura-okoshi*'s "main emphasis is action rather than research or planning."

I observe the following three aspects of *mura-okoshi* in the conventional local development discourse in Japan:

1) *Mura-okoshi* as a social movement: Among many Japanese, there is a sympathetic feeling for the case in which a locality resists conventional metropolitan- and industry/large corporation-based development power. In this sense, some (mostly Japanese mass media) may tend to see *mura-okoshi* as a social movement, for which there are very few academic interpretations. It is appropriate to conclude that counteracting conventional national and regional development regimes, as well as the global economic system, is one aspect of *mura-okoshi*.

2) *Mura-okoshi* as a political tool: Goto observes that there is "bureaucratic zeal for 'soft' or cultural administration partly reflecting the increased interest of private corporations and individuals on non-metropolitan affairs" (1993: 17). With the growing interest in and awareness of *mura-okoshi*, the government and politicians have tended to support and institutionalize—or politicize—it within conventional subsidy-based policy measures.[23] Today a great number of national subsidy programs for rural areas are available, which could possibly be effective external financial sources for rural development and, at the same time, could be effective political tools for politicians.

---

22 Goto uses a term chiiki-okoshi (regional revitalization), which has basically the same meaning as mura-okoshi.

23 For example, the Prime Minister Takeshita's 100 Million-Yen Grant Program for Countryside Renaissance (Furusato Sosei Ichi-oku-yen Kikin). Through this program, the national government grants 10 Million-yen (about US$0.8 million, at the current rate) to individual municipalities as an open-purpose subsidy for local development.

3) *Mura-okoshi* as alternative development: Some see *mura-okoshi* as the practice of alternative development connected with the concept of regionalism (localism) and contrasted with conventional growth-oriented development theory. There are five significant characteristics of this normative concept, as defined by the Dag Hammarskjöld Foundation. It is (1) need-oriented, (2) endogenous, (3) self-reliant, (4) ecologically sound, and (5) based on structural transformation (Nerfin: 1977: 10, quoted in Hettne 1995: 177). There was a boom of *mura-okoshi* in its alternative development aspect in Japan from the mid-1980s to the early 1990s, which brought certain rural development actions to light and which contributed to increasing general public interest in *mura-okoshi*. During this period the mass media, policy makers, and some scholars were eager to support and sympathize with this seemingly "alternative development" practice.

While I do not deny the possibility that some rural development practices actually possess the above-listed characteristics, at the same time, I must voice my skepticism about making utopian claims for *mura-okoshi*, such as those that were common in certain mass media.

CHAPTER 3
GUNMA PREFECTURE AND
RURAL VILLAGES

3.1. The geographical setting of Gunma Prefecture

Like the greater Tokyo metropolitan area, the Gunma Prefecture is located in the northern fringe of the Plains of Kanto. Gunma Prefecture developed in a polarized way. On the one hand, the central-southern part of the prefecture is significantly urbanized; economically it is directly integrated into the Tokyo metropolitan area. This is due to its flat topography and easy access for commuting to the Tokyo region. Maebashi (the capital city of Gunma; population 283,000) and Takasaki (the economic center of the prefecture; population, 239,000) are the two major cities. They are adjacent to each other and function as twin cities. On the other hand, most villages and towns, especially those in the northern and southeastern parts of the prefecture, have become economically depleted and depopulated due to their mountainous topography, poor non-farming employment opportunities, less productive small-scale agriculture, and—up until the 1980s—poor transportation. This is despite their relatively close location to the metropolitan areas. Although they are hilly and mountainous, these villages are not totally isolated today. It takes only two to three hours to get to Tokyo from the villages by *Shinkansen* train or highway, both of which came into service after the 1980s.

With the exception of Ogo township, which is now functioning as a suburb of Maebashi, rural localities for this study were chosen from this region of Gunma. All localities, except Ogo, include the hilly and mountainous areas, defined by the Japanese Agricultural Census as agriculturally less favorable, or handicapped topography, in their territory. A detailed description of each village and region will be given later in the chapters in which the case study is presented.

I must note that, with respect to socio-economic decline and "backwardness," Gunma villages (except Ueno in this study) are still in a much better position than those in other regions, such as Hokkaido, Chugoku (western part of the main island), and Shikoku (the fourth largest island facing the Pacific Ocean). In the mountain villages of Shuikoku and Chugoku, which are geographically and economically more remote from major metropolitan regions, the local economies are becoming weaker, and, year by year, villages are disappearing due to excessive depopulation and the aging of the remaining population. Gunma's situation is probably not as serious. Rather, we can appreciate that its location gives the people certain advantages for dealing and communicating with outside towns and cities.

From another point of view, however, their relative proximity to the metropolitan region means that they are always exposed to the temptation of commercial-based mass development. I think this contradictory situation makes Gunma (and rural municipalities there) one of the more interesting examples of rural development in Japan to investigate.[24]

3.2. Changing spatial-economic environment affecting Gunma localities

In the following chapters, I will describe and examine the effort for rural development and preservation in six cases: Sawada, Kawaba, Niiharu, Ueno, Kurabuchi, and Ogo, all of which are rural localities in Gunma, Japan. In general, these six rural localities began at the same point, three to four decades ago, as villages of sericulture, small farming, and forestry.[25]

The globalization of production and trade has dramatically changed Japan's industrial structure, including agriculture and forestry. The market liberalization of silk products, timber, and farm products caused the loss

---

24 Roughly speaking, historically, eastern Japan (with the exception of Hokkaido—the North Island) was developed with paddy farming, in which a strong communal ties in many aspects of village governance and people's living have been developed through irrigation and water management practices. Such communal functions include ceremonies of marriages and funerals, and communal operation of paddy farming and forestry. On the other hand, western Japan was developed with upland cropping -based agriculture, in which communal functions are less tight, due to the absence of water management practices. Geographically, Gunma is in eastern Japan. Although not a pure paddy oriented region, it still possesses some characteristics of a paddy-based society (Odagiri, interview on July 24, 1998).

25 Except the township of Ogo with respect to forestry.

of the traditional economic bases of these six villages. In addition, Japan's rapid industrialization during the 1950s and 1960s served as a catalyst for a massive migration of the agricultural populace from rural areas to the cities and industrial districts surrounding them. This dramatically reduced the population of the above six rural localities.

During the time of low economic growth (1980s until the present), each of these six localities has taken a different direction, both economically and demographically. This is due to their own internal response to these forces and struggles for development, and due to the changing geography caused by the influence of urbanization, suburbanization, and the global economy. Some of these localities have successfully preserved their ruralness by inventing ways to attract urban money. Some have been "engulfed" by a powerful wave of urbanization. And others have been—and are—continually losing the economic basis for their existence (Figure 1).

3.3. Japanese villages

In this book, I use the English term, "village," as the translation of the Japanese term, *mura*, referring to a locality, or community, located in a rural area.

The Japanese word, *mura*, can refer to a village as a modern municipality or to one in the traditional sense. There are, thus, two meanings of *mura*. In the first, or original, meaning, *mura* refers to a community or hamlet (*buraku*, in Japanese) where close kinship and communal ties have been maintained. In the past, it was not only an autonomous socio-economic unit with a physical boundary and including farmland and forest (often communally owned and operated), but also a political/administrative unit (during pre-modern times). In the second, or contemporary meaning, *mura* is mainly used to refer to a form of a political/administrative unit. In the following chapters, when I use "Kawaba village" or the "village of Kawaba," I will be using *mura* in the second sense.

Villages, towns, and cities are Japanese municipal units representing the lowest administrative authority. They are basically distinguished according to population: a village has a population of 5,000 or less; a town has a population of 5,000 to 50,000; and a city has a population of 50,000 or more. A village usually can be divided into several administrative districts or *aza* which, in some cases, are former municipal villages merged into a current, bigger village. These old villages include several hamlets or *buraku*, which sometimes can be considered natural villages.

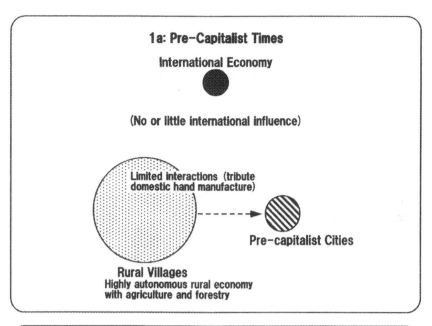

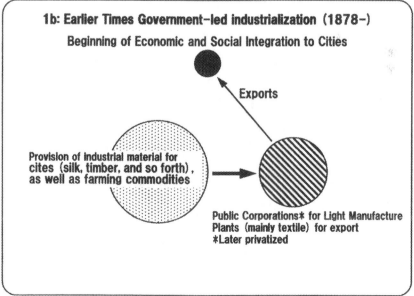

Figure 1: Historical Evolution of Rural Place Differentiation and Spatial Integration in Japan

Figure 1 (Continued)

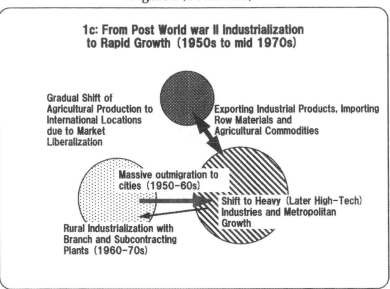

1c: From Post World war II Industrialization to Rapid Growth (1950s to mid 1970s)

Gradual Shift of Agricultural Production to International Locations due to Market Liberalization

Exporting Industrial Products, Importing Row Materials and Agricultural Commodities

Massive outmigration to cities (1950–60s)

Rural Industrialization with Branch and Subcontracting Plants (1960–70s)

Shift to Heavy (Later High–Tech) Industries and Metropolitan Growth

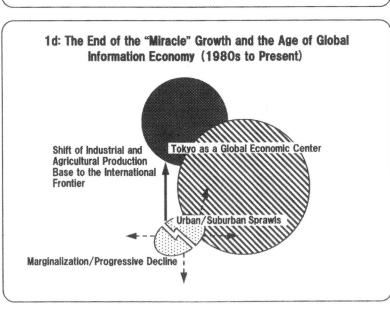

1d: The End of the "Miracle" Growth and the Age of Global Information Economy (1980s to Present)

Shift of Industrial and Agricultural Production Base to the International Frontier

Tokyo as a Global Economic Center

Urban/Suburban Sprawls

Marginalization/Progressive Decline

Hence, a village in the latter meaning consists of a relatively large spatial territory. Besides those areas of residential hamlets, the remaining physical space is farmland or forest. Therefore, the spatial area of a Japanese village is typically greater than that of a U.S. village. For example, the area of Niiharu village, one of the six cases studied for this book, is 182km²; 84% of its area is covered by forest.

As the lowest governmental unit, a municipality has a municipal government (which is also referred to as a "village/town/city office" or "local government" in this book) headed by an elected mayor and a municipal assembly.[26] Even a small village in Japan, as a municipality, has an elected full-time mayor, a village assembly with elected members, and a village office with a bureaucratic organization with full-time employees and professionals, including planners. Its administrative capacity is relatively well organized, compared with that of a U.S. village.

The Japanese national government has been promoting the consolidation of municipalities, especially those rural villages and towns with poor economies and/or those that are sparsely populated. Consolidation saves administrative costs, including those of public servants, as well as subsidies/financial assistance from higher government authorities (national/prefectural). For instance, Sawada, one of the six cases in the study, was an independent village until 1955. It was then merged with two other villages into an adjacent town, Nakanojo. Thus, if the population of a village decreases significantly, thereby reducing tax revenue to the village office, the rural village would be faced with the critical decision of whether to stay independent or to become part of a financially wealthier municipality (in most cases a neighboring city/town) via merger. This is one reason that many rural municipalities in Japan view maintaining population and especially the settlement of younger productive people as a top priority rural development policy issue.

---

26 In the Japanese government/political system, there are three levels of government: the central/national government, consisting of ministries and agencies headed by ministers with cabinet status and the diet (congress) with upper and lower houses; prefectural governments headed by an elected governor and a prefecture assembly; and municipal governments headed by an elected mayor and a municipal assembly.

CHAPTER 4
MAPPING SOCIAL AND ECONOMIC TRENDS IN GUNMA PREFECTURE

In this chapter, I present a number of indicators of social, economic, and spatial trends for rural communities in Gunma Prefecture. These trends are mapped. The maps, together with qualitative information contained in the following chapters, assist in understanding the situation of Gunma villages in the broader perspective of social, economic, and spatial change. They demonstrate uneven development in progress.

First I present maps of Gunma Prefecture that show its location, topography, administrative sub-units (municipalities), population density, and the location of the six localities chosen for in-depth case studies. (Figures 2 to 5).

Demographic changes

Gunma has seventy municipalities: eleven cities, thirty-three townships, and twenty-six villages. In general, it is commonly understood that cities are urban areas characterized by high concentrations of population and primarily non-agricultural land uses; villages are largely rural, sparsely populated, and with primarily non-urbanland land uses; and townships are intermediate between the two in terms of population and land use.

The reality, however, is not so simple. A series of municipal consolidations has made official demographic statistics less useful for the purposes of this classification. Most municipalities are a mix of urban and rural with respect to

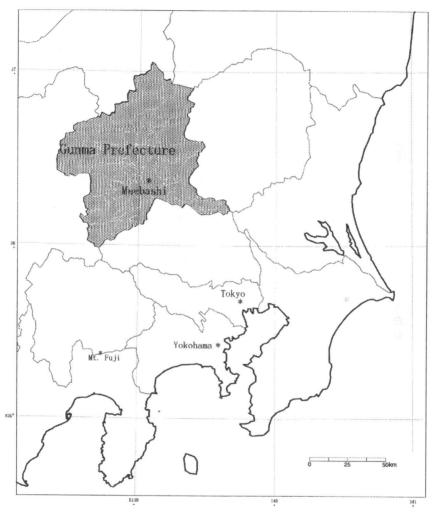

Figure 2: The Kanto Region

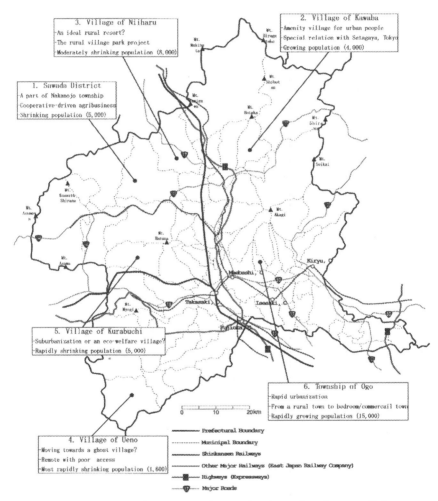

Figure 3: Gunma Prefecture and the Six Case Study Localities

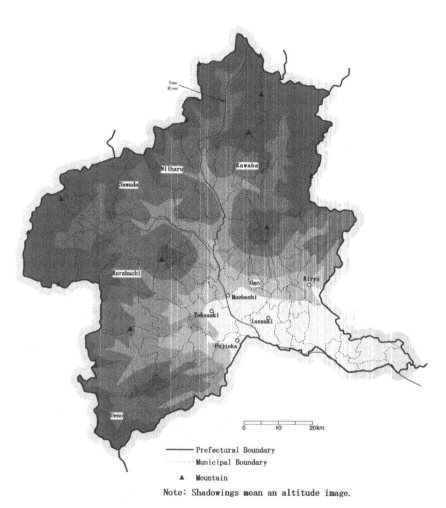

Figure 4: A Topographical Image of Gunma

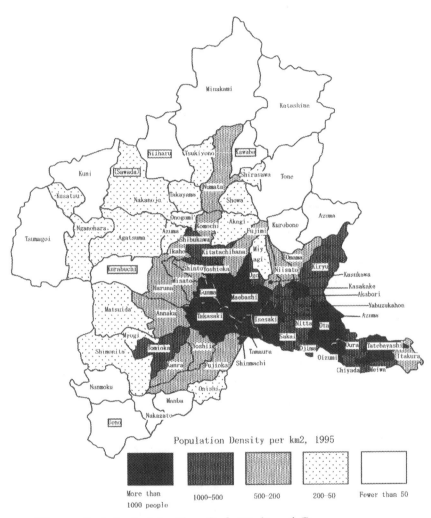

**Figure 5: Administrative Sub-Units of Gunma
(Municipalities) and Population Density**

land use and population concentrations. For example, in the city of Fujioka, which has a long, narrow shape (see Figure 5), the core city area is located in its most northern part, adjoining Takasaki; the rest of Fujioka's territory (about 60% of the area) has characteristics similar to those of a rural or mountain village. Likewise, some townships and villages with low population densities have a relatively high proportion of non-agricultural land use. Official statistics for municipalities do not reflect these sub-area differences within municipalities, i.e., low-population density areas within urban municipalities and high-population density areas within rural municipalities.

With respect to trends in the total population of the prefecture, from 1985 to 1995 Gunma's population grew by 4.3%. However, as shown in Figure 6, this growth is uneven throughout the prefecture. Growing municipalities are mainly located in the southern portion of the prefecture, which is part of the Kanto Plain. All cities in the prefecture, with the exception of Kiryu, grew. However, the greatest growth in population did not necessarily take place in cities. For example, population growth in the cities of Maebashi and Takasaki, Gunma's traditional commercial (and political) centers, was nearly stagnant (2.7%) during the decade under examination, while certain townships and villages (such as Ogo) surrounding the two cities experienced rapid suburban-type population growth. As described in the chapter on Ogo, unchecked suburban sprawl and mixed urban-rural land use are becoming more apparent in this region. More remote municipalities in hilly and mountainous regions experienced rapid declines in population although in this, too, there were exceptions, such as Kawaba (growing) and Niiharu (declining, but at a moderate rate). In seven municipalities, including Ueno, Kurabuchi, and Kawaba, the aging population (65 years and older) is greater than 25% of the total population; most of these municipalities (with the exception of Kawaba) experienced a rapidly shrinking population.

In sum, suburban sprawl and peripheral decline are very general demographic trends in Gunma.

Two factors contribute to a region's population change: natural growth and social changes. Natural growth is the difference between births and deaths. Social changes impact in- and out- migration. Overall, the Gunma population increased by 48,442 people during the period from 1991 to 1995 (Gunma Prefecture 1997). This increase was due to a positive balance between new births and deaths (27,378)[27] and to a net in-migration of 21,064 people.[28]

---

27 99,765 new births versus 72,387 deaths.
28 237,886 in-flows versus 216,822 out-flows.

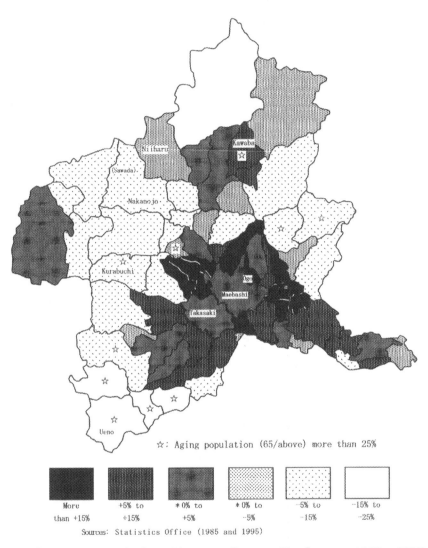

☆: Aging population (65/above) more than 25%

| More than +15% | +5% to +15% | * 0% to +5% | * 0% to -5% | -5% to -15% | -15% to -25% |

Sources: Statistics Office (1985 and 1995)

Figure 6: Population Change, Gunma Prefecture 1985 - 1995

Figure 7 presents a summary of intermunicipal population outflows between 1991 and 1995. Migration outflows from municipalities with a net positive in-migration are not shown here. An arrow indicates quantity and direction of the greatest intermunicipal population outflows for municipalities having greater population outflow than inflow. Municipalities having greater inter-prefectural outflows (outflows to other prefectures) than internal outflows (outflows to other municipalities within Gunma) are highlighted. It is reasonably assumed that these out-migrations are mainly to Tokyo.

It is clearly observed that population outflows from rural municipalities are to neighboring urban municipalities, while some more remote rural municipalities (such as Kusatsu and Minakami) and some major urban municipalities (such as Takasaki and Kiryu) have greater out-migration to other prefectures than they do internal migration within the prefecture.

Per capita income

As shown in Figure 8, in 1995 there was spatial inequality in per capita income between urban municipalities and rural townships/villages. Average per capita income for all of Gunma Prefecture was 3,098 thousand yens. This is lower than the national average of 3,118 thousand yens.[29] In general, high per capita incomes within Gunma were concentrated in and around major cites, such as Takasaki, Maebashi, and Isesaki. In addition, there were some scattered, relatively high income villages and townships in the more remote, hilly and mountainous regions, such as the townships of Kusatsu and Minakami (both well known for having the most popular *onsen* resorts). The wealthiest municipality was Takasaki with a per capita income of 3,803 thousand yens, and the poorest was Shirasawa with a per capita income of 1,769 thousand yens.

Japan is, of course, one of the wealthiest economies in the world; and so, even the per capita incomes of the poorest villages may seem high compared with those in the remainder of Asia and in other Third World regions. Nevertheless, in the context of Gunma, rural communities in hilly and mountainous areas are peripherized to some degree with respect to per capita income.

Growing service sector employment

It is necessary to offer some cautionary notes at the outset of a discussion of changes in service sector employment. One must be aware of the limitation of official statistics in terms of offering an understanding of the skills associated with jobs in this sector. The service sector, as defined in the Japanese population census, is that sector not included in agriculture, forestry, mining, manufacturing, and construction sectors. Within the service sector, there are

---

29 The wealthiest prefecture is Tokyo (4,225 thousand yens); the poorest is Okinawa (2,149 thousand yens).

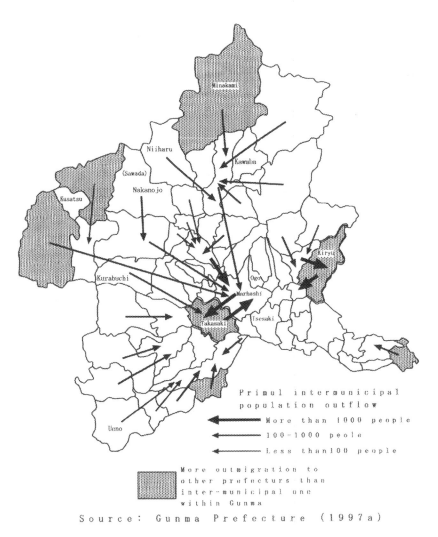

Figure 7: Major Out-Migration Flows 1991 - 1997

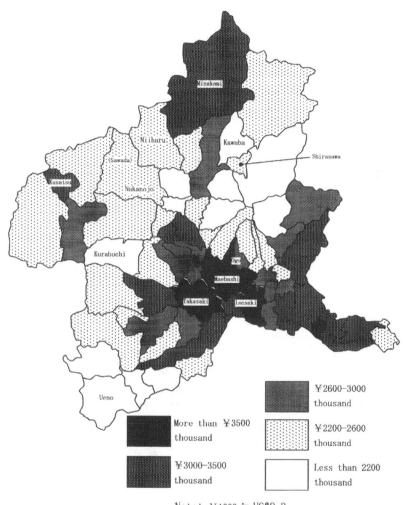

Figure 8: Per Capita Income, Gunma Prefecture 1995

seven large industrial sub- classifications: (1) utilities (electricity, gas, and so forth), (2) transportation and communications, (3) wholesale, retail and food service, (4) finance and insurance, (5) real estate, (6) other personal services, and (7) public services. Service sector jobs include both knowledge-intensive and labor-intensive jobs, and both skilled and unskilled labor. Although, in the context of industrial structural change, it is common to attribute increases in service sector employment to advancements in knowledge-based technologies (such as telecommunications and biotechnology), and therefore to think of changes in service sector as representing increases in high-skilled jobs, this cannot be inferred from Japan's official employment statistics on service sector employment. If the focus is high-skilled knowledge-intensive jobs, these occupations may be present within other industrial categories, as in the R&D sector of the manufacturing industry. Conversely, service sector jobs may range from those with very low skills to those with very high skills.

Although ideally I wanted to look at changes in skills or occupations, these data are not available in Japan. The data presented here are service sector employment data, and hence should not be confused with data relating to skills. Overall, total service sector employment (excluding public service employment) in Gunma Prefecture grew from 431,507 to 534,177 over the decade from 1985-1995. I have excluded public service employment (i.e., civil servants, fire, police, post), because increases in public service employment could reflect policy responses to economic decline, as in the case of Ueno, which used increases in public service employment to offset losses of jobs in other sectors (see Chapter 9).

Figure 9 presents growth in the share of service sector employment from 1985 to 1995 in Gunma. In 69 municipalities out of 70, service sector employment grew over that period. The increases in major urban municipalities with traditional business districts were relatively low (Maebashi, Kiryu, Numata, and so forth). The only municipality in which the share of service sector employment decreased was Takasaki. The figures rose most rapidly in some seemingly economically suburbanized municipalities (Takayama, Tamura, Kawaba).

Locational changes in manufacturing

During the decade from 1985 to 1995, total employment in manufacturing in Gunma decreased slightly, from 298,262 to 297,721. The number of factories with more than three employees fell from 9,843 to 9,120, while the number of factories with more than 300 employees increased slightly, from 103 to 110 over the same period.

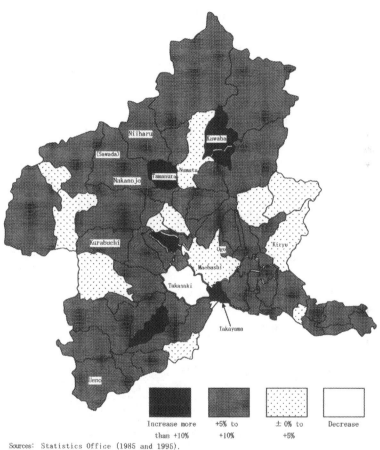

Sources: Statistics Office (1985 and 1995).

Notes: (1) Civil servants and public services are excluded.

(2) Subtraction of the share (%) of service sector employment in 1985 from the same
figure in 1995, but not the percentage change in real numbers of employment
between two years.

Figure 9: Changes in Service Sector Employment 1985 - 1995
(Changes in Percentage of Total Employment)

Figure 10 shows the geographic trend in number of factories. The number of factories decreased in 36 municipalities out of 70. I must, again, note that these statistics do not distinguish knowledge-based, high-tech activities from other types of manufacturing. The data show that, as a general trend, small, typically family-operated subcontracting factories are declining in significance as a conventional industrial basis in many areas, including rural communities.

There are three major trends in the distribution of factories in Gunma. First, the number of factories decreased at a relatively high rate (losses of between 10 and 20%) in major urban municipalities, such as the cities of Maebashi, Takasaki, Kiryu, Tomioka, which have long been industrial centers of the prefecture. Municipalities with over 100 factories in 1995 are distinguished on the map with an icon. Clearly, in most of these municipalities, the number of factories is dropping. Second, many of the more remote rural municipalities, such as the villages of Kurabuchi, Nakazato, Kuni, also lost factories at a high rate. Third, the remaining municipalities, most of which are rural municipalities and townships, experienced an increase in the number of factories. If we compare Figures 3 and 10, we will observe that the latter municipalities are typically located along major expressways and roads (with some exceptions—including Ueno[30] and Manba—both of which are located in Tano County).

To summarize, although no large change was observed, it is appropriate to conclude that conventional manufacturing is gradually declining in significance as part of the local economic base, or at least that massive growth in conventional manufacturing can no longer be expected in rural Gunma.

Declining agriculture

In general, there are reasons for pessimism about the future of the farm sector in Gunma. This is not only due to external pressures for market liberalization of agricultural commodities, but also due to internal "collapse." A few figures are enough to explain this critical situation. As shown in Figure 11, during the decade from 1985 to 1995, the number of farms (farm households) declined in all 70 municipalities of the prefecture. A remarkable geographical trend is that the loss of farms was by far the greatest (more than 30%) in mountainous rural regions, including the villages of Ueno, Nakazato, and Nanmoku, in which there is also a significant aging of the

---

30 In Ueno, there were nine factories in 1995, all of which were small-scale with less than eleven employees; whereas the same figure was seven in 1985. Since two newly added factories have fewer than four employees, I assume they are small woodcraft-related ones being promoted by the village.

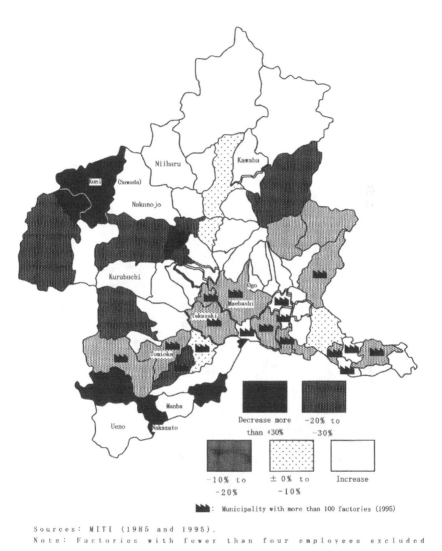

**Figure 10: Change in Number of Manufacturing Plants
1985 - 1995**

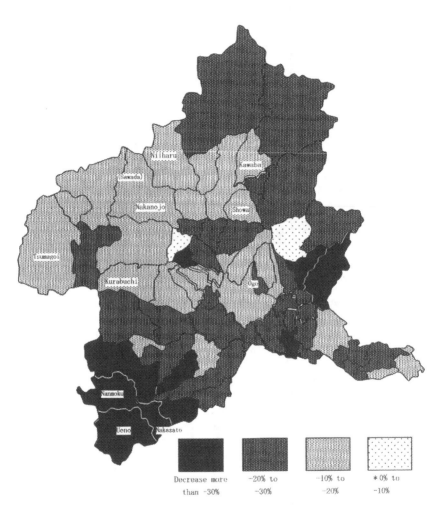

**Figure 11: Change in Farm Numbers (Farm Households)
1985 - 1995**

population as well as significant population loss due to massive out-migration to cities. Major urban municipalities and surrounding suburban townships and villages, where the pressures for leaving agriculture (because of growing demands for land for non-agricultural uses) are expected to be large, show the second highest number of farms lost (between 20 and 30%).

Generally, Japanese agriculture's scale of operation is extremely small. In the case of Gunma, the average size per farm (household) is only 89 ares.[31] Even in such villages as Tsumagoi and Showa, where agriculture is relatively large-scale, the average size is only 336 and 253 ares, respectively. For this reason, I do not include large-scale, highly productive, commercial agriculture in the future scenarios for rural development in Gunma.

Social services and infrastructure

People cannot live without jobs, but people cannot live on jobs alone. In order to provide for people's basic needs, quality social services are essential. To examine the geographical disparity in such services, I present the distribution of educational and health-related service facilities in Gunma (Figures 12 and 13).

Distribution of these facilities is largely urban-biased. There are 38 municipalities, most of them rural municipalities in more remote locations, without senior high schools. For the high school age population in some of these locations, such as the villages of Ueno and Nakazato, it is difficult—or nearly impossible—to commute from their villages to schools in urban municipalities. In Gunma, as in all of Japan's prefectures, all four-year universities are located in metropolitan regions.

With respect to health care facilities, there are 35 municipalities without hospitals (small clinics and similar kinds of facilities excluded). If we compare Figures 12 and 13, the patterns of the geographical distribution of high schools and hospitals are strikingly similar. Those municipalities that lack a high school also tend to lack a hospital.

Information infrastructure and services

Finally, the geographical distribution of information services and infrastructure is critically important for regional economic development as we enter the age of the information society and the global economy. The 1997 White Paper of the Japanese Ministry of Post and Telecommunications (MPT) offers a useful measure of these variables—the Regional Information Intensification Index (RII Index)—as well as a means to study their distribution in Gunma. The RII Index is a score representing the degree of provision of an information

---

31 1 are = 100m².

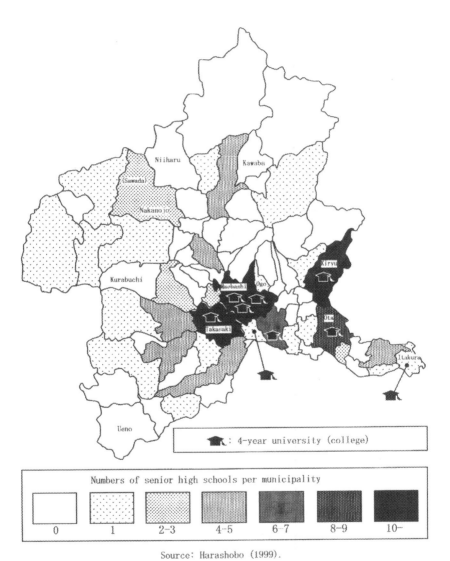

Source: Harashobo (1999).

Figure 12: School Locations

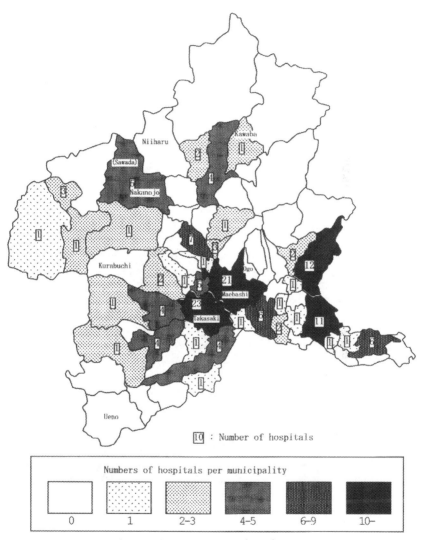

: Number of hospitals

Numbers of hospitals per municipality

0	1	2-3	4-5	6-9	10-

Source: Gunma Prefecture (1999b).

Figure 13: Hospital Locations

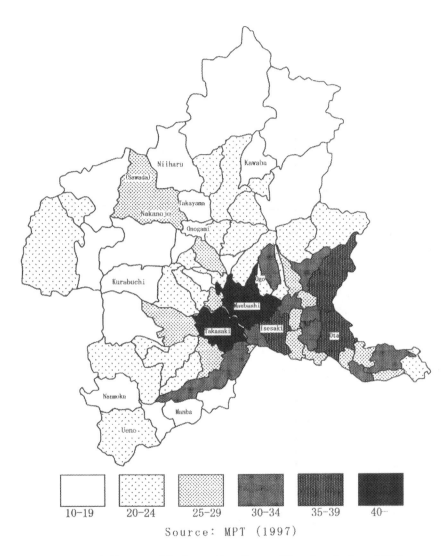

Source: MPT (1997)

Figure 14: Regional Information Intensification Index, 1996

infrastructure and the availability of information technologies in public services in all Japanese municipalities from Hokkaido to Okinawa. Scores (0 to 3) are given for each of 37 items relating to information services and infrastructure, such as availability of an ISDN, fiber-optic cable (main access points), mobile phones, CATV, and so forth. These are summed as the RII Index (MPT 1997).

The maximum score on the RII Index is 89 and the minimum is 0. Among all 3,255 municipalities in Japan, the municipality earning the highest score (68 points) is the city of Fukuoka (Fukuoka Prefecture on the Kyushu Island), which is well known for IT-related investment. As for average scores by prefecture, Tokyo Prefecture has the highest score (39.9). Gunma's average is 24.4, which is slightly higher than the national average of 22.4.

Figure 14 presents the distribution of the RII Index in Gunma. The highest score is 43 points for the cities of Takasaki and Maebashi, followed by Isesaki and Ota with 37. The lowest scores were in the village of Takayama (10), followed by the villages of Onogami (13), Nanmoku (14), and the township of Manba (14). Even in the cities with the highest scores, ISDN services, or high speed data access via fiber-optic cables, are not available in all districts—only in some limited parts of the cities; and most of the existing public services are not yet on-line. In villages which scored the lowest, conventional telephone service is available; however, more up-to-date information services are not, and there may even be difficulty in listening to FM broadcasting. The distribution of higher scores is heavily urban- or, more accurately, metropolitan-biased.

PART TWO

ANALYTICAL DESCRIPTION

CHAPTER 5
NOTES ON METHODOLOGY

In the following chapters, I will explore the research questions I listed in Chapter 1 by examining information gained from field interviews and from my own observations. Basically, each locality is described, examined, and analyzed according to the following format:[32]

(1) INTRODUCTION: A brief overview of the present state of the locality, as well as economic, demographic, and social trends from a historical perspective are presented in order to introduce the village to readers;[33]

(2) POLICY PERSPECTIVES (PLANNING POLICIES): A description of significant development and village revitalization planning using empirical information based on document research and interviews—mainly of planning officials;[34]

(3) CITIZENS' PERSPECTIVES: An examination of citizens' response to—and a preliminary evaluation of—these *mura-okoshi* efforts based on interviews

---

32 With the exception of Kurabuchi and Ogo.

33 To consider the social and economic status of a locality and its change, it is not enough to perceive the locality in a 'parochial' way—i.e., from a single viewpoint—based, for example, solely on data restricted to the political boundaries of the municipality, as Massey (1993) argues. While I essentially agree with this view, I believe it is still appropriate here to provide readers with information and figures on the settings of the case based on the existing 'parochialism.'

34 In this section, a planner refers to professionals involved in policy planning, including not only village officials, cooperative officials (for the case of Sawada), and professional consultants/scholars, but also in some cases local politicians, such as mayors and assemblymen.

with villagers and, in part, planners' explanations. Also, an examination of distinctive features and factors that affect the locality's performance; and

(4) CONCLUDING REMARKS: An analysis of (a) the reasons for successes/ failures of development efforts; (b) the present functioning of the locality, and the directions I believe it will take—or be forced into—from a long-term perspective, assuming that the current policy intervention continues.

Although this is the general format, the means of presenting information for each case is not uniform. Rather I employ different approaches in order to present effectively and accurately my research on diverse, case-specific performance.

CHAPTER 6
A COOPERATIVE AS AN ENGINE FOR LOCAL ECONOMIC VITALIZATION?

6.1. Introduction

One of my case studies is the former village of Sawada. Sawada village was formed in 1889 by the merger of five originally smaller villages, which are, today, residential sub-districts within Sawada. The village of Sawada was an independent municipality until 1955, when it was merged with two other villages into the township of Nakanojo, following the enactment of the Municipal Consolidation Promotion Act of 1953 (*Choson Gappei Sokushin Ho*). Today, Sawada is a part of Nakanojo, which is located in the northwest region of Gunma.

The area of what was once Sawada village is 166km². The topography is hilly and mountainous. Forests cover about 86% of the total area; residential areas (including *onsen* resort areas), about (11%), and farmland (3%). If you were to drive R353 from the town center of Nakanojo to Sawada, you would see that the landscape changes dramatically upon entering Sawada. In the 1940s the population of Sawada was nearly 8,000. By 1995 it had decreased to 4,795. In the last two decades population in Sawada declined by 4 to 6% every five years.

Agriculture and *onsen* tourism are the major industries in Sawada. Like other villages in the region, prior to the rapid economic growth period local people were mainly engaged in farming and forestry in a highly self-sufficient way, combining livestock and field crop production, such as vegetables and rice, and sericulture. In the 1960s, with the enactment of the Agricultural Basic Act of 1962, selective agricultural specialization was promoted as a national agricultural policy. In Sawada it was decided that farmers should specialize in hog raising and sericulture. However, the specialization policy failed due to weak competitiveness of Japanese silk in the global market and unstable prices in the pork market. Today about one third of Sawada's 1,500 families are farm households, most of which are small-scale and with an aged population.

Sawada has a long history as a traditional *onsen* resort since the discovery of hot springs there in 989 (Arisue 1993: 121).[35] Two *onsen* districts in Sawada (Shima *onsen* and Sawatari *onsen*), with about 60 inns and hotels, have annually attracted 400,000 to 500,000 people[36] in recent years. Shima *onsen* is the fourth largest *onsen* in annual revenues in Gunma. Since the end of the Bubble Economy in the late 1980s, Sawada's *onsen* industry has experienced a decrease in both the number of guests and profits, and is now undergoing hardship due to the current bad economy.

6.2. Description from a policy perspective

"Our village revitalization begins with building local industry. Build our business for earning stable incomes! " (The basic slogan in the Sixth Five-Year Plan (SAC 1997); translated by the author).

In this section, I describe Sawada's development efforts. Although the name, Sawada, disappeared from the map, Sawada is well known because of the Sawada Agricultural Cooperative (SAC), which, over the past three decades, has been deeply committed to local development and agricultural promotion using a unique agribusiness/tourism strategy. Under SAC, business has successfully expanded. A key individual in the organization has provided vigorous leadership and played a critical role in planning and implementation. Because SAC represents the primary development initiative in Sawada, it plays a central role in this chapter.

---

35 For Japanese people, onsen, which can be translated as a spa or hot spring, does not have the same meaning as spa resorts in western cultures. Onsen tours have always been major parts of Japanese popular resort and recreational life. Generally onsen spots are located in many mountainous regions and form resort areas. Sugiura and Gillespie explains, "Onsen heal the body and nature heals the mind and heart" (1994: 192).

36 This figure includes tourists who come just for an onsen bath at inns/hotels, but who do not stay overnight.

The Sawada Agricultural Cooperative

Today, there is no major industry besides agriculture and *onsen*-tourism in Sawada. Most farmers are part-time, aged, and female. Agricultural production takes place primarily for domestic consumption rather than for the market. Before the 1955 merger, there was an agricultural cooperative in each village. Following the merger, these cooperatives merged into one larger cooperative. This cooperative covers two municipalities, including Nakanojo and Agatsuma townships. Today SAC is formed with about 500 farm households and has 40 of its own full-time employees.[37] This is the only cooperative in the Nakanojo township (the Town of Nakanojo) that has existed as an independent *nokyo* up until this day without a merger.[38] In Sawada, SAC has a unique development philosophy and strategy and has played a powerful role in planning and local development initiatives.

Introducing new businesses: The first five-year plan

In 1972, SAC developed its first five-year plan, which included an agricultural processing plant project operated by the cooperative. It was Kastuya Seki, the Chief of Planning for SAC at the time, and presently its executive manager, who elaborated this idea and persuaded the executive manager at the time to implement it, despite opposition from all other employees. Since then, Seki has been a powerful and influential leader and key person in many aspects of Sawada's development. Seki recalls,

---

37 In Japan, agricultural cooperatives (nokyo) are another huge bureaucracy, especially in rural regions. They were formed by the national government with the Agricultural Cooperatives Act of 1947 (Nogyo Kyodo Kumiai Ho) to promote the economic benefit of farmers and their families through programs of credits, cooperative shipment/purchasing services, technical/managerial advice. A three-tiered hierarchical organizational structure is developed with three-levels of administration: 1) headquarters (national level), 2) prefectural offices (prefectural level), and 3) municipal cooperatives (local level). However, the local cooperatives are basically assured independence from higher authorities in management. They provide services to their community, but are never merely branches of prefectural-level organizations. These days, agricultural cooperatives, especially local ones, are severely criticized by farmers, the media, and others, due to poor services, commitment, and a bureaucratic mentality. SAC should be regarded as one of the exceptionally "good" local cooperatives with respect to management and a deep commitment to serving farmers and promoting the community.

38 Also, many local cooperatives are having managerial problems, and cooperative mergers/consolidations are being enforced.

"I made a draft plan entirely by myself. All the board members disapproved, saying, it's a revolution. It's unrealistic. We cannot do this. But I was lucky that an executive manager told me, let's do it" (Interview).

Under this plan the cooperative began to produce *tsukemono*—Japanese pickles and saltings, one of the essential and popular foods in the Japanese diet—at a SAC processing plant.[39] This was successful because of excellent product quality and taste, and because of a local-based marketing strategy.

SAC now consistently produces and sells about 130 items. The food (mainly pickles and saltings) business was highly successful and brought a huge profit to this small cooperative. Annual sales of the food business grew steadily until 1990, and since 1990 annual sales have been 0.5 billion yen or more, despite a recent decline in demand due to the current recession.

Selling locally

Ever since the beginning, for the most part, SAC has never advertised its products. Originally it was the member farmers and cooperative employees who spoke about their pickles and saltings to the locals, thus spreading the word. Then local people began to use their products as gifts and for social events, such as weddings and funerals (Nobunkyo 1994: 18).[40]

Generally, SAC products are sold only locally or through mail order. There are two *nokyo*-shops in the village. Some local gift shops and hotels also sell SAC products. There are three contracting shops in other urban locations in Gunma Prefecture. And SAC owns one satellite shop in Kita City of Tokyo, in order to survey urban consumers' response to their products. That's all.

As the fame of SAC's product quality grew, major department stores and supermarkets offered SAC deals to sell its products in major metropolitan centers, such as Tokyo. The cooperative rejected all such offers. In order to maintain quality, the cooperative decided to stick to small-scale operations and not to take the route of mass production in order to sell at supermarkets. SAC's product quality relies on freshness, which means that it processes vegetables and fruits immediately after the harvest, without any additives (Nobunkyo 1994: 17).

Also there is a consumer preference for these products because of their scarcity value in the market. Seki speaks of this as follows:

---

39 Most funding for building the plant came from subsidies from the Ministry of Agriculture.

40 In most Japanese social events, including weddings and funerals, a gift for the participants is very common. This custom of gifting can be found in every aspect of social relations.

"Well, as far as we sell locally, local people buy and outside visitors also buy when they come here. But, if our products were available in department stores in Tokyo, no one would pay attention to them. You know they're selling all kinds of food from all over Japan, no, from all over the world. Do you see what I mean? That's why we restrict ourselves to the area for our business" (Interview).

Regarding price, Sawada's food products have never been priced at less than similar kinds of food produced by major food industries. But local people prefer Sawada's foods, according to Seki. He is very proud of his marketing strategy and the quality of the products.

From agricultural promotion to local economic development: The fifth five-year plan

While earlier plans saw agricultural promotion as the sole principal task of the cooperative, in the fifth five-year plan of 1992, titled "The Challenge (*chosen*)," SAC defines a new role for itself as an actor to promote local development through building a new economic foundation based on agribusiness and tourism. The basic recognition was that, regardless of the success of the food processing business, Sawada faced a number of problems commonly found in Japanese agriculture and rural areas, including depopulation, an aging population, and a decline in the number of full-time farmers. To cope with this situation, SAC decided to add new businesses in order to promote local development.

Presently, SAC is promoting both an herb business and tourism development. The cooperative built a theme park called *Yakuo-en* (The Kingdom of Herbs) in 1996. The park promotes the basic concept of "health," which is now the people's biggest interest in Japan—just as it is in the United States.[41] The park includes herb gardens, an herbal-food restaurant, shops, handicraft art schools, an herb pharmacy, and nature trails. A Chinese herbal physician has been invited to give visitors advice about the use of herbs. An agreement with the Herb Resources Research Institute at the Chinese University of Medical Sciences in Beijing was signed in order to obtain technical advice and cooperation.

The primary economic objectives of the park are the promotion of herb-based agribusiness and tourism, greater sales of Sawada products, and the creation of new employment opportunities. Seki told me that it is desirable for SAC to support economically 70% of the local people, including non-farmers.[42] Farmers produce ingredients for Sawada products. People in *onsen-*

---

41 Today, herbs are experiencing a kind of boom among health-conscious people in Japan.

42 Including direct employment and indirect support such as the distribution of the profits of the food business to cooperative members.

tourism hotels and shops sell SAC products. And SAC provides non-farmers with places to work at its plants and at the theme park. In order to persuade farmers to participate in herb production, which was quite new to them, SAC first conducted its own experiments in cultivation, processing, and tasting.[43] After it had collected scientific data, it asked farmers to join.

SAC now sees agritourism as a future development option. It considers the *Yakuo-en* park (the herb and agritourism theme park) as a showroom for SAC businesses and as a tourist attraction center. Today, there are 250,000 visitors to the park each year, which is slightly short of making a profit.[44] Yamada, a SAC official, states that it is probably too early to evaluate this new challenge.

Planning "by ourselves," the planning philosophy

Seki emphasizes "ownership" of planning and implementation for their projects. He maintains,

"I don't trust people like professors and consultants. They are of no use. In their mind, theories always come first [in their planning practices], such as preservation of the environment and local culture. It's beautiful, but do the environment and culture feed us? In my practice, an economic policy, in other words generating income opportunity, must always come first. Otherwise people leave this place. …We never use outside consultants for planning [of our mid-term plans]. They have no responsibility in actual implementation. They merely come from Tokyo to draw a plan, using statistical data and theories, and go back when it's done; you know, just like they do in any other place. It's us, our employees and farmers, who work and live here. …If the people working here plan by themselves, we can feel satisfaction with our job" (Seki, Interview).

The Fifth Five-Year Plan was developed through a unique process of communications. In mid-term plans, an aim or goal is stated, and it is supported by definite objectives with more detailed operational and implementation plans. At the very first stage of development of the plan, staff and employees in each division of SAC discuss and draw up a draft idea. A planning committee organized with eight employees with a special appointment examines and combines ideas from each division and sections it together as the very first draft of the plan.

---

43 Essentially the experiment is the responsibility of the local extension center. However, SAC actually conducted experiments itself. Regarding this, Yamada maintains, "they have no responsibility. That's why we did it by ourselves" (Interview).

44 According to Yamada, at least 350,000 visitors per year are needed to make a profit (Interview).

When SAC developed its fifth plan, which was the turning point for the cooperative and local farmers, there was an impasse, and no novel ideas for a breakthrough came from the participants at the very beginning. Then Seki ordered all employees in a managerial position, including relatively young ones, to visit and see other municipalities or *nokyo* from Hokkaido to Okinawa in Japan. They then had a meeting to exchange ideas and discuss what they had seen and learned outside Sawada. Seki ordered them to bring their own ideas for another presentation session.

Seki is proud that this process facilitates and greatly promotes a sense of participation and responsibility among SAC employees. As the first draft was shaped, it was fed back to farmers through community meetings (*buraku-zadankai*), which are held twice a year (spring and fall) between SAC and all districts (hamlets) in Sawada. Based on feedback from farmers, further revisions were made in the plan, which were then presented again to the farmers for their feedback. These communications between SAC and the community occurred five times until the Final Plan was finally approved.

"We've just done an exact job for our member farmers. That's all. For three decades, our firm mutual trust between the nokyo (SAC) and member farmers has been developed in this way"(Nobunkyo 1994: 78)

New business fitting local situations and traditional farming practices

Indeed, SAC is responsible for buying all commodities that farmers produce regardless of quality, quantity, or market prices. This means that SAC assumes all risks in farming for their farmers. One of the main aims of the project is stabilization of members' income, thus reducing the risk of specialization. SAC assures member farmers a fixed price for vegetables for processing.

In Sawada, many farmers, especially women and the elderly, are farming mainly for their own consumption, and not for the market. Hence they produce a wide variety of crops in small quantities, rather than specializing in a single crop for the market. When farmers owned livestock, they sometimes fed the animals with the surplus crops, but they no longer do this. A female farmer says, *"Today, the nokyo buy any crops the member farmers produce, even with very small quantities. I really appreciate it"* (Nobunkyo 1994: 30).

In addition, most vegetables for pickles and saltings, such as myoga, udo, and scallions, naturally do not require chemicals and are easy for women and elderly farmers to harvest because they are not heavy (Nobunkyo 1994: 22-23).

In Sawada, what livestock remain provide farmers with manure for natural fertilizer, which is essential for vegetable and fruit farmers in order that they have improved harvests in their small-scale operations (Nobunkyo

1994: 24-25.). This was widely practiced before the 1970s when each farmer engaged in livestock production, field crops, and sericulture, and utilized the manure from their own livestock.[45]

A charismatic leader

Without Seki's ideas and initiatives, SAC would never have performed as well as it has. Truly, Seki is not only an executive member of the cooperative, but he is also a devoted and farsighted local leader and rational businessman. Seki utilizes strong connections with bureaucrats in the central government,[46] perhaps with the mayor of the township who used to be his boss in SAC, and even with a Chinese university. However, while Seki's strong leadership is clearly a strength, it could also be a weakness for SAC. There is a danger in SAC relying solely on one particular individual.

Yamada, SAC's Planning and Development Chief, observes that, compared with farmers in other districts of Nakanojo township, Sawada farmers seem submissive. This he believes is because of the presence of the cooperative and its powerful leadership (Yamada, Interview). Seki emphasizes the role of a cooperative or local government in organizing people to follow a path of agricultural and industrial (primarily local agribusiness) promotion and development. Seki stresses the leading role of an existing organization such as *nokyo* or local government, and he also emphasizes the importance of leadership by one particular individual within the organization.

"There are a few farmers who are trying to promote their farming operation with their own ideas in a sporadic manner. But how can they be successful? They are too limited in knowledge and resources. In the old days, there was a traditional-type leader in the village who took leadership, and everyone followed him. As village governance is democratized, there has not been such an individual today" (Seki, Interview).

Seki apparently believes that the village still needs a powerful local leader, and probably believes that he should be that leader.

---

45 Livestock farming dramatically declined after the 1970s due to the rise in feed prices caused by the oil crisis. This coincided with the decline of sericulture, and, as a result, the self-production of organic manure disappeared (Nobunkyo, 1994, pp.25-26).

46 Seki is serving as a member of various deliberation councils for the Ministry of Agriculture and maintains connections with the ministry's executives. He calls the ministry's executives and negotiates with them before the municipal government officially applies for subsidies. Nevertheless, I do not believe this works all the time; it may be true that his personal network affects actual practices of acquiring outside resources, including funding and knowledge, in many ways.

SAC now has rich experience in agricultural processing and a local sales strategy, but its new herb business relies on capricious preferences of urban consumers. Therefore, Seki emphasizes the importance of unceasing efforts in R&D to develop new ideas and products as the only way to deal with changing trends in consumer demand.

An engine for promoting Sawada community?

SAC's initiatives began three decades ago in an effort to sustain Sawada's small farming community, despite forces generated by changing state and global economic and social situations. SAC then expanded its efforts to local economic development projects based on local agriculture and agritourism. From one standpoint, SAC has been successful in adding new businesses to the local economic base, including an agri-theme park, and in promoting small agricultural communities in this mountain village. Local government has supported this strategy:

"There are five important fields in local economic development, they are agriculture, commerce, manufacturing, forestry, and tourism. All are equally important, but equally decline. As a government, we should treat them equally, but if I give a priority, I would say linking agriculture and tourism, then commerce will be benefit" (Shinichi Sekiguchi, Planning division, Nakanojo township Office, Interview).

What has made Sawada's effort successful? How and to what extent does it—and will it—affect the broader picture of development of the Sawada communities in both an economic and social context? Who benefits? Who does not? In what direction is the village heading? SAC executives see their organization as both a powerful vehicle for local economic development and a system for distributing welfare to the community. To what extent are its goals attained? What is the future direction of the Sawada community?

6.3. Evaluation from a people's perspective

Before I conducted field interviews with local people and other SAC employees, I was simply hoping to find that SAC would be a good model for achieving sustainable development—for effectively utilizing existing local resources, with older farmers, in small-scale subsistence farming. And I expected that what made Sawada's effort exceptionally successful and durable would be its powerful leadership from a few cooperative executives. Regarding leadership, my hypothesis was strengthened by interviews with other cooperative employees and with villagers. Interviews with local people made me think that Sawada is also exceptional in geography.

However, as a result of my research, I have developed skepticism with respect to the sustainability of current Sawada efforts and with respect to the cooperative itself.

The purpose of this section is to present my observations and evaluation, based on data and information obtained from field interviews with 34 Sawada people, in order to answer the above questions.

A successful business enterprise

The emphasis within SAC shifted from merely selling locally produced and processed, quality foods for the promotion of Sawada agriculture to economic activities that attract urban money. The cooperative executive calls this a "shift from agricultural promotion to local economic development," and he see their projects as "regional development." I see SAC as an institution with two functions: first, as a money making enterprise and, second, as a cooperative distributing benefits to local people both directly and indirectly. Sawada, today, is widely regarded, in both the popular media and academic publications in Japan,[47] as one of the successful and lasting *mura-okoshi* efforts.

Viewed from a business perspective, SAC's market strategy is reasonable. Today it produces more than 40 food products, and its sales are consistently $5 million per year.[48] Its business strategy, although contrary to that of large food enterprises producing and selling their products through the mass market, gives a small farmers' cooperative some strengths in the market. In addition to this market strategy, one of the strengths of SAC is its effort in R&D. Seki says that consumer interest in processed foods such as those produced by SAC lasts no longer than three years. Thus SAC needs to invest constantly in developing new products. SAC employs technical specialists, such as food scientists and pharmacists, and consults with Chinese professors; these efforts contribute to technical competitiveness in new product development. Recently, SAC hired an R&D and marketing expert who previously worked for one of the major companies in the Japanese food industry. He told me,

"One of SAC's advantages is it develops a clear view (on business). Compared with other nokyo (agricultural cooperatives), it has been maintaining a critical sense of crisis traditionally. ...It's blessed with good human resources and leadership. ...It's possible to expand the current sales 5% without a significant change in the way of business. But, I think we need to expand our sales 20 - 30%, to improve

---

47 For example, Takahashi (1985), and Nobunkyo (1994).

48 Total sales of processed food in 1995 amounted to 706 million Yen (approximately $5.9 million at a rate: $1 = 120 Yen).

the level of living standard... as a quasi-enterprise" (Osamu Watanabe, R&D specialist, SAC, Interview).

As we have seen above, with respect to employment, the importance of SAC for community economic development is significant. It is obvious that without SAC and its economic development strategy, Sawada would never be as it exists today. For example, in 1995, Sawada had a population of 4,795 with 1,560 households. Of these, 500 households are members of SAC.[49] This means that approximately one-third of Sawada dwellers are directly benefiting from SAC's activities, although the degree of benefit varies greatly according to types of—and commitment to—farming. In addition to this, SAC has created employment opportunities in food processing plants and in its theme park (approximately 60 full-time and 40 part-time employees).

Local economic vitalization, or just a welfare program?

However, I must point out that, in terms of creating a firm economic basis, SAC has limited impact in the whole picture of Sawada's regional development. First, those who most enjoy a direct economic benefit are small-scale, aged, retired farmers who are engaged in subsistence farming and sell surplus products to SAC. SAC assures these people an income in addition to their pensions. Second, it is primarily women, especially housewives, who benefit from additional income opportunities as laborers for SAC or as farmers.[50] In this sense, SAC may be seen as a welfare policy for the elderly and female, rather than an economic development project for the whole region.

Out of the 500 farming households in Sawada, only 100 are full-time farming families. The rest rely on off-farm earnings in manufacturing, commerce, construction, *onsen*-hotels, or in the public sector. This means that the majority of Sawada dwellers earn their incomes in non-farming sectors and/or commute to downtown Nakanojo or other neighboring localities. For these people, Sawada is functioning as a bedroom community, although the meaning of the term for Sawada residents is not the same as that for residents of bedroom-towns or satellite cities of Tokyo.

SAC officials emphasize that SAC's food processing plants and theme park provide not only direct benefits to member farmers, but also employment opportunities for non-member local people, especially the elderly and female. These officials are proud of SAC's role in sustaining the local economy. Public opinion on this varies greatly depending on commitment to—and involvement in—SAC activities. Overall, among my interviewees, it was

---

49 This number is declining as the average farmer's age increases.
50 It is typical, in most part-time farm households in Japan, that wives are mainly engaged in farming, while husbands work in a non-farm sector.

cooperative employees along with aged and female small-scale farmers who most enjoy SAC's direct benefits and welcome their programs:

"I can maintain my livelihood in Sawada with farming, because of pension. This is a good place to live" (Takeshi Seki, farmer, 69 years old, Interview).

Unlike these "hobby" farmers, professional farmers engaged in agriculture on a full-time basis comment differently:

"Farmers are relying on SAC too much. They believe it's OK if you only listen to what Mr. (Katsuya) Seki said" (Hiroshi Saito, Farmer, 42 years old, Interview).

"I, as a professional farmer, am not interested in the SAC business. ...Farmers have no chance to know the market value of their products. It makes farmers just subcontractors. Farmers don't know what's going on as a whole" (Tohichi Tamura, Farmer, 59 years old, Interview).

"The presence of the cooperative has been too big so that farmers are totally relying on it. There is no room for farmers' will and attitudes or self-development under such a SAC-led environment" (Kazuhiro Yamaguchi, Farmer, 43 years old, Interview).

Ironically the SAC plant and business does not have the capacity to accept a larger quantity of products from relatively big farmers like Yamaguchi. He thus continues,

"It's unavoidable. Larger farmers, like me, do not use SAC" (Yamaguchi).

Thus, SAC's activity relies on small subsistence and/or "hobby" farmers in Sawada. However, because SAC's initiatives for promoting agriculture and the local economy have never been powerful enough to stop the decline of Sawada agriculture, SAC will lose its presence in the community. As of 1995 there were 1,560 households in Sawada, of which approximately 500 were farm households; whereas in 1975, 665 out of 1,366 households were farmers. Although an exact figure is not available, aging is going on in the Sawada community, especially among farmers. For demographic reasons the presence of farmers in the community will decline dramatically in the next one or two decades, regardless of SAC's development efforts.

"Realistically speaking, I see the tie between SAC and its 500 member farmers gradually getting weaker. The community won't need SAC. Farmers are becoming part-timers. There is a limit to what a farmers' cooperative can do" (Tamura, Interview).

SAC, of course, recognizes this situation, and if the answer is further investment in new economic activities such as the theme park and herb business described earlier, Katsuya Seki and SAC employees predict,

"Sawada will be a village without agriculture. Such a village with no industry will disappear in mountainous regions, or will be housing and industrial areas in flatter regions" (Katsuya Seki, Executive Manager, SAC, Interview).

"Young populations are leaving not only from Sawada, but from all of Nakanojo. No one can stop it. We need employment opportunity here, and it's (our agri) tourism." (Takaichi Karasawa, SAC, Interview).

"Our foundation is processed farming products, providing real foods. ...Health, environment are our essential keywords. We promote those to feed the Sawada community with our agricultural products. We will act differently from mass-production business" (Soichi Seki, Food plant manager, SAC, Interview).

Non-farmers' view

How do non-farming people, the majority of Sawada residents, see SAC activities? In general, most non-farming people I interviewed have positive impressions of SAC, because the name "Sawada" has acquired some degree of fame. People naturally feel happy that their village is well-known for something. However, many of them actually have little or no interest in SAC programs. An *onsen*-hotel owner in Sawada feels that SAC makes little contribution to the rest of the Sawada community, including those who are in the *onsen*-business community and own local retail shops. Both the hotels and retail shops are having difficulty due to the current economy and—with regard to retail shops—due to the growth of big supermarkets or discount shops brought by sprawling suburbanization in neighboring urban localities.

"SAC never sells vegetables wholesale to local retailers. Everything goes to their plant to be processed, and they sell only at their own shops. ...SAC is an organization that makes farmers lazy. There are too many controls over farmers. ...It's an enterprise. ...It's no good, even for agricultural promotion" (Fumio Yuasa, Hotel owner, Interview).

"I have no interest in what SAC is doing at all. ...There are more people who are no longer farming here. ...I welcome development and suburbanization from which a good price and nice goods are available to us. A big factory and shop will be more welcomed for job opportunities. ...I have no relationship with mura-okoshi. More people are coming to Sawada (because of SAC's mura-okoshi), but this only makes SAC rich. I really wish for local development. The best thing is job opportunity for everyone (who wish to stay here)" (Masayuki Ishida, Branch plant worker in a neighboring township, 37 years old, Interview).

To summarize, how the local people view SAC differs greatly according to their degree of involvement in SAC, or, in other words, the extent of their direct economic benefit. Regardless of these negative responses from villagers in local businesses, SAC's role in local economic development, and in preserving Sawada's rural identity, through three decades of development should not be underestimated. However, as I have confirmed through interviews, there is a limit to what a farmers' cooperative can do for local development. In this sense, it is not like a government agency or mass-production industry.

Changing geography surrounding the community

Is Sawada a good example of successful local economic development in a small mountain village, which many see as a geographically handicapped or disadvantaged area?

First of all, is Sawada disadvantaged—economically, locationally, or geographically? As I was pursuing a number of interviews in Sawada, one Cornell professor's words came to mind, "I don't like the phrase 'handicapped area,' which some people tend to use. There are no handicapped areas, in a true sense" (Greenwood 1998, Personal communication). Greenwood explained that a community with a disadvantage in some aspects does not mean it is entirely disadvantaged in all aspects. Some Japanese scholars who tend to view rural areas mainly from the perspective of agricultural production may see Sawada as (agriculturally) disadvantaged due to its mountainous topography. I basically agree with this view. However, as my interviewing went on, I developed a conviction that this village is not disadvantaged with respect to non-agricultural economic opportunities, even at the present time. This is contrary to my earlier biased view of Sawada as a mountain village.

As mentioned earlier, the current municipality, the township of Nakanojo, was formed in 1955 by the merger of three rural localities, including Isama village, Nakuta village, and Sawada village, with the original Nakanojo township. Before World War II, the county government, which no longer exists today, was located in the original Nakanojo, which now functions as a commercial and residential district. Nakanojo's commercial community, which consists of traditional, small-scale retailers, is becoming less active year by year. There is a neighboring locality that is eager to pursue economic development with external commercial and industrial capital. In Haramachi district of Agatsuma township, a municipality adjacent to Nakanojo, branch plants have been invited and large-scale commercial development projects have been promoted for years. After the 1980s, improved road infrastructure enabled Sawada residents to have convenient access to the Nakanojo and Haramachi districts. Today, from any of the 18 hamlets in Sawada, it takes only 15-30 minutes to commute to these industrial and commercial districts by car. And from Sawada, it takes only 90-120 minutes to be in Maebashi city, the prefectural capital, and Takasaki city, the prefectural economic center where many urban conveniences are available. Indeed, among my Sawada interviewees, which included over 30 people, very few feel economic or psychological isolation or remoteness. Rather, most expressed some sense of integration between Nakanojo township and the capital/metropolitan region of the prefecture, which is about a 70-90 minute drive:

"I don't see any inconvenience in living in Sawada today. We have vehicles and telephones. The only exception is hospitals. But living in Sawada today is much more convenient than it was in the old days. There might be a lot of nice places outside this community to be in, but I love living here" (Takeshi Seki, Farmer, 69 years old, Interview).

"It's not very inconvenient if you drive. I do most shopping in Nakanojo township, and sometimes go to Takasaki or Maebashi city. Prices are low here. We have warm neighborhoods. My daughter, who studied at a university in Chiba and worked in Meabashi for a while, is coming back here and now works in Nakanojo" (Kumiko Karasawa, Housewife/Farmer, 58 years old, Interview)

"In terms of psychological distance, I feel it is very close to cities. It takes only one hour or so to get to Takasaki. I have no sense that I'm in a remote community" (Nobuo Miyazaki, Manager, Shima *Onsen* Association (Chamber of *Onsen* Hotels), Interview).

"Jobs are available within a distance not beyond Takasaki and Maebashi (cities) for Sawada people. Most people today are wage workers, and Sawada is economically no longer a rural village (in a pure sense)" (Toshikazu Namiki, SAC employee moved from Yokohama 5 years ago, Interview).

"I don't feel a strong desire from students that 'we want to get out of here,' due to its rurality" (Shunichi Kanai, High school teacher, Interview).

Where is Sawada's economy headed?: future directions

In response to my question on the ideal functioning of the village in the future, almost all people desire to preserve the countryside's current landscape with farmland and forest. They also wish to maintain a stable population, especially with younger people to vitalize the community. Some say it is contradictory to have both, while others say it is possible.

There are three different views on the future direction of Sawada community, which I would call optimistic, pessimistic, and realistic. Among 15 respondents to this question, there were three optimists who dream of a possibility for Sawada agriculture:

"Thirty years later, farming will be operated by entrepreneurs. SAC's food processing and herb processing will progress and will be big. ...Even if high productivity (in farming) and good income are assured, successors (of agriculture) will be maintained" (Takaichi Karasawa, SAC, Interview).

"Desirably, lots of tourists will come to Yakuo-en (the theme park) and Sawada. Tourism programs will be successful, and farming products will be sold" (Toichi Tamura, Farmer, Interview).

"I didn't expect the era of automobile, or even airplane to come so soon. ...As Lester Brown says in his books that I've read, I presume another society, where the basic value is not economically-oriented, will come in the near future" (Rikio Yamada, Farmer, Interview).

On the other hand, eight pessimists all point out that the current demographic trend, in which the loss of young population is prominent, will continue unless the region has other industries, other than farming and related business, that can offer employment opportunities for the young.

"Getting smaller. SAC will be too small or become merged. It's unavoidable. Unlike places where large farmland is available, it's impossible here. No factories. Young people leave for cities. That's the only way" (Takamatsu Iizuka, Farmer, Interview).

"Economy will get worse. Fewer tourists. Onsen will be worse-off. ...To keep young people, we need companies and factories that pay good salaries" (Shoji Yoshinari, Chef for a *onsen* hotel, Interview).

Finally, there were four realists who anticipate the further suburbanization of Sawada as the transportation infrastructure is improved and the further decline of SAC and agriculture.

"We are heading towards suburbanization. There'll be more big supermarkets. Farmers will be dying. The local retail community should be transformed into a place where tourists can enjoy walking, watching, and shopping. ...Local residents want conveniences so that suburbanization should be unavoidable. ...The future economic vitalization should be double-functioning (local residents enjoy suburban life, whereas Sawada keeps tourist-attraction charm). ...But we need to hold onto Sawada's identity" (Fumio Yuasa, *Onsen* hotel owner, Interview).

"In the districts adjacent to the town center of Nakanojo, urban sprawl, which converts farmland into a housing district, is in progress. ...The whole population around Shibukawa city (including Nakanojo/Sawada) is not shrinking. We are already entering into the greater Tokyo metropolis. If a planned new freeway connecting Shibukawa and Nagano runs to Agatsuma (a neighboring town), it will only take two hours to get to Tokyo" (Shinichi Sekiguchi, Planning division, Town of Nakanojo, Interview).

"To consider Sawada's development seriously, we should discard the view that Sawada is rural. There are landscapes of countryside and, in this regard, I could say it's rural, but economically it is no longer rural. ...I believe we need to preserve our paddies, farmlands, and forests, not for the purpose of economic activities, but as environmental policy. We should invest in this. ...(As for development) there should be a variety of job opportunities that can afford a range of people with varying educational background (from unskilled to well-educated) within the area of a one-hour-drive. That is essential" (Shunicshi Kanai, High school teacher, Interview).

As the above high school teacher pointed out, Sawada is economically no longer a rural area in a traditional sense, and the planner sees that it is located on the fringe of the great metropolitan region. According to what I feel is the realistic point of view, Sawada will not be able to hold a stable economic foundation based on agriculture and its rural character. However, economic security can probably be assured for Sawada residents through suburbanization. In this case, can Sawada preserve its rural identity?

Yes, I believe it can. But again, as the high school teacher mentioned, it is another issue over which SAC may have no control.

6.4. Concluding remarks

We now have discovered a difference between what executives of the Sawada cooperative believe and what local people feel and believe about agribusiness/tourism projects and the future development of Sawada. We also found diverse opinions among local people on SAC, depending on the interviewee's age, occupation, educational training, and commitment/loyalty to SAC and its program. My own view is that while I agree that there are limits to SAC's policy from the perspective of comprehensive local development, nevertheless, I believe that SAC has played a powerful role as engine in the promotion of the local economy,

Under the distinctive leadership of a cooperative executive, SAC, through its efforts in local economic development has sustained the agriculture and farming community, including farmland and rural landscapes in Sawada. These comprise a major portion of Sawada's rural identity. Small-scale, subsistence agriculture has been preserved and the skills of aging farmers effectively utilized.

I have observed that SAC's success is due, to a large extent, to two major factors:

1) *Leadership*: Due to SAC's distinctive efforts and leadership, Sawada is assured an economic foundation other than agriculture (onsen and branch plants included) within the region, including neighboring localities. If SAC and its executive's remarkable leadership and initiatives for such programs had not been available, the life of the majority of its members would be worse-off, and this would have led to further economic devitalization and depopulation of the Sawada community. In this sense, SAC has been successful in preserving rural identity and promoting economic development.

2) *Onsen*: Sawada's *onsen*-resort is relatively small and not well-known, unlike some of the other major Gunma *onsen* resorts. Obviously, without *onsen*, SAC would not have been successful in selling its foods and in attracting tourists to its park. Although both SAC and the *onsen* want to have more shared visitors, I believe that the impact on further local economic development of these sectors must necessarily be limited, because these economic activities employ only a limited number of people.

I would argue, however, that leadership and the presence of *onsen* are what I will call "exceptional" factors—that is, they are unique to Sawada. For this reason, I conclude that SAC's success as a development model cannot necessarily be generalized to other rural areas.

Even within Sawada, I would argue that SAC will play an ever declining role in Sawada's economic future, due to *changing geography*. In the past, Sawada's economy was based only on farming and *onsen*. That was everything. Now Sawada is located on the fringe of sprawling suburbanization. It is directly connected to other urban localities in Gunma and to the greater Tokyo region. Since roads have significantly improved, the people of Sawada can commute to neighboring localities where some acceptable jobs are available. However, most of these are unskilled (blue-collar) jobs in branch plants and construction firms. Whereas the village still possesses a traditional spirit and communal ties, it is, however, economically-speaking no longer an agricultural-based village.

Sawada is functioning as a bedroom community, even though the degree of that is moderate compared with urbanized communities surrounding Tokyo. While the majority of interviewees want to preserve their countryside (rural identity), they told me they also wanted a firmer economic basis (employment opportunities, especially for skilled labor). In this regard, there is a limit to what an agricultural cooperative can do.

In conclusion, what is SAC's role in the future development of Sawada? Can SAC with its agritourism save Sawada's independence from the effects of ongoing changes in economy, technology, and geography? Can SAC's initiatives attract younger people to the community, which is essential for stopping an aging town population? A number of interviewees anticipate "it cannot." I agree that it can't. However, as a *nokyo* (agricultural cooperative) SAC has no other choice but to continue with what it has been and is doing—not only for local development, but also, ironically, for sustaining itself. Given the rapidly changing spatio-economic environment, the cooperative has no other choice but to adhere to its place-based practices.

Assuming that the present social, economic, and spatial trends continue, and assuming the absence of a strong policy/planning intervention that would alter the course of current trends, I see two possibilities for Sawada's future: 1) to be a bedroom community with a few hobby farmers; or 2) to experience a general increase in the number and proportion of the aging and a gradual decrease in total population, meaning that, over time, the community will die out.

CHAPTER 7
AN AMENITY VILLAGE FOR
URBAN PEOPLE

7.1. Introduction

Government programs directly aiding poor people and communities in non-metropolitan regions are often not successful. However, sometimes a community or locality can develop a capability for coping with social and economic problems by establishing links with well educated middle-class people—making use of their knowledge as well as their financial and political resources (Clavel and Goldsmith 1973). For example, as Clavel and Goldsmith point out, there is some evidence of middle-class participation in local actions and development efforts in the cities and small towns of Upstate New York in the United States. This chapter describes the example of a non-metropolitan locality's development effort that utilizes both the resources and the expertise of middle class people from outside the region.

The village of Kawaba, in Tone County, is located in the northern part of the Prefecture. The area of the village is about 85.3km², and it spreads over the south slope of Mt. Hotaka whose altitude is 2,158 meters. About 85% of the village territory is forest, followed by farmland (7%) and housing (1%). Due to poor access to the metropolitan regions, before the Post World War II period of rapid economic growth, Kawaba was a sort of isolated mountain village. Villagers depended, in a semi-autonomous manner, mostly on small-scale, highly-diversified, mixed agriculture, sericulture, and forestry. Just as in other rural villages in this region, sericulture was the most important source of income. Villagers also produced rice and konyaku potatoes, and they raised livestock and other food crops, basically for domestic consumption. Today Japanese sericulture has almost died out due to a drastic decline in Japanese sericulture and the silk industry. And Kawaba will never be able to have large-scale productive agriculture, due to its socio-economic situation and topography. Today (1995), about 600 farm households in the village cultivate 600ha of farmland for apples, rice, livestock, vegetables, and many other crops.

Employment in the agriculture, manufacturing (food processing, sake breweries, and small subcontracting manufacturing), and commerce/service (including public services) sectors in Kawaba is 31%, 26%, and 43%, respectively. About 40% of the working population commutes—chiefly to the city of Numata (an adjacent urban municipality with a population of 47,000). This means that the number of out-commuters from Kawaba is highest among the first five cases of this study (with the exception of Sawada, for which the figure is not available).

Transportation access to Kawaba from Maebashi/Takasaki and the Tokyo region was dramatically improved during the 1980s with the opening of the Kanetsu Expressway (1985) and the *Shinkanen* (1983). Today it takes 2.5 hours to drive, and 1.5 hours by *Shinkanen*, from Tokyo.

The population of Kawaba, according to village records, was about 4,000 in the early 18th century; in the mid 19th century it had fallen to about 2,500 (Nakajima 1992: 46). In the time of modernization after the *Meiji* Restoration (1868), it grew consistently, reaching a peak of 5,376 in 1955. After World War II, population decreased to 3,822 in 1975, the lowest on record. However, in the past two decades, Kawaba's population has grown at a moderate rate. It was 4,274 in 1995.

7.2. Description from a policy perspective

Kawaba has been successful in both economic development and in maintaining its rural character by employing a unique local development policy. According to the current mayor, Yokoasaka, there was a growing sense of crisis in the community when the village was experiencing declining population and losing its economic foundation during the late 1960s. For revitalizing the village, local political leaders (chiefly the mayor) envisioned the future of their village to be one which accommodates urban people on holiday vacations (Hashiguchi 1996: 213). At the time there was still little awareness of vacation and recreation in Japan.

In the following, I offer a brief historical sketch of Kawaba development and policy planning by using the explanations of a village planning official I met.

Agriculture and tourism for urban dwellers

From one perspective, agriculture is still the principal industry in Kawaba, although it is in decline. About one half of all its families are farm households. Minoru Miyauchi, a planning official for the village office, views agricultural promotion as critical; however, it should not be conventional agricultural development.

"Well, here it is impossible to develop our agriculture in a way for mass production of a single crop, which some neighboring villages are doing. Yet, we need to protect our agriculture. Why? We must assure the farmers income through preserving our country landscape with an agricultural practice" (Interview).

He believes a beautiful countryside is a resource that can be used to attract urban people to visit this mountain village. And Kawaba's rural landscape, comprised of rice paddies and traditional silk-farmer-style houses, has been —and can be—maintained only through active farming and a farm population. In this view, farming is not merely a means for producing food, but it is a critical part of the rural landscape. "Agriculture and tourism," a phrase that originated with the late Mayor Tsuruji Nagai, has been a keyword of Kawaba's development strategy.

Mayor Nagai, a unique and revolutionary man

As the political leader of Kawaba during the period between 1968 and 1983, Nagai was "a unique leader and a highly energetic man," Minoru Miyauchi recollects, and continues,

"He was originally an owner of a local sake brewery. We rarely saw him in the village hall. He liked traveling, touring around outside the village. He traveled to many places in Japan, and even outside Japan. In fact, he was outside the village 2-3 months a year, cumulatively. Every morning there were a lot of people in line in front of the mayor's room to have his signature on their documents before the mayor went out. ...There were three village leaders including him running for elections. But Nagai never lost. ...It was Nagai who proposed to build a hotel with a secondhand train—a steam engine with three sleeping coaches—in the village. Everyone except him opposed his idea, 'cause we thought no one would come to such a country place like this. But he built it. And it was the beginning" (Interview).

People at that time thought that the village was nothing but an agricultural settlement—that there was nothing to attract outside people, and, hence, no one would visit such a place. This was just after the rapid economic growth period of the 1950s and 1960s and after the oil shock.

It is a fact that, at that time, there was little awareness among Japanese of spending leisure time in rural areas. When a village-owned train hotel opened in 1977, the expectation was that it would have 50,000 visitors a year. Presently, 600,000 people come annually. Following the hotel, a convention facility, historical museum, and some other activities were added, with financial support from the central government.[51]

"Nagai always maintained a close communication with influential individuals in the village who had been policy advisors to him and appointed them to be members of various councils and committees for the village" (M. Miyauchi, Interview).

Nagai retired from his position as mayor to run for the Gunma Prefectural Assembly in 1983. The current mayor, Yokosaka, his successor, is following Nagai's policies. Miyauchi says *"He opened our eyes, and we learned that it can be changed if we do something."*

Rural-urban partnership programs

In the late 1970s, the city of Setagaya was looking for a rural municipality for a partnership program and for *Kenko-mura* (translated as the Village of Health—an exchange facility allowing Setagaya residents, especially school children, to stay in the countryside). Setagaya has the largest population (773,000 in 1999) among the municipalities in the Tokyo Metropolitan Prefecture and is well-known as a residence for a number of famous artists, sports stars, and scholars. In addition, it is well known for its consumer activist movements. Basically it is not an industrial district, rather it is known as a mostly residential and educational district. In fact, there are eight universities in the city.

Kenko-mura was one of the top seven policies decided on in 1979 in a 10-year development plan for Setagaya. For this project, in the same year, under Mayor Ohba's initiative, the Setagaya office established a special working committee with expert planners chaired by Tadayoshi Suzuki, professor of urban planning at the Tokyo Institute of Technology. Based on careful deliberations, in 1981 the city finally, out of 52 candidates, chose the Village of Kawaba for its partnership, The selection was based on a number of criteria, including the environment; topography; accessibility; cultural/historical heritage; availability of local manpower and medical services; local government policies; willingness to cooperate; and friendliness. Kawaba was chosen from the final five candidates because improvements in transportation—the

---

51 According to M. Miyauchi, 70-80% of spending for this purpose comes from government subsidies and other forms of financial support from the central government. This is a commonly found budgetary arrangement in poor rural municipalities and is sometimes criticized as hojokin-baramiki (reckless subsidy spending).

Freeway and *Shinkasen* which were already being constructed at the time (CDC 1985: 143-144), assured its accessibility.

In Japan, it is common for many rich metropolitan municipalities to have facilities, like hotels or condominiums, opened exclusively for the residents of the municipalities. Setagaya's concept was different from others, as Miyauchi maintains: *"Their concept of Kenko-mura and their entire concept of a rural-urban exchange program was very different from conventional ones."* Watanabe (1984: 265), a colleague of Professor Suzuki at T.I.T., summarizes the three main objectives of the program:

1) For Setagaya, it provides urban dwellers a place to enjoy rural amenities not simply as a tourist resort, but as a *furusato* (a native place, home);

2) For Kawaba, it provides the village and villagers a business opportunity, voluntary manpower (from Setagaya) for forest preservation and other activities, the opportunity to enjoy urban culture and entertainment in Setagaya; and

3) For both, it provides possibilities for further expansion of the program and relations for future development.

As Miyamuchi recalls: they were not merely seeking a place to build a hotel-like facility for their citizens; rather they were looking for a long-lasting relationship with rural people, which would be beneficial for both the urban and rural dwellers, and which would be a true second *furusato* for Setagaya dwellers. Now, as extracurricular education for the 5th grade elementary school children in Setagaya, a total of 27,000 children stay in Kawaba for three days every year in the spring and fall.

Instead of choosing to build one huge accommodation facility, which would have minimized construction costs, Setagaya chose two different building locations in Kawaba. This was done because one huge building would have been inappropriate for Kawaba's landscape, plus this approach generated greater job opportunities for citizens of Kawaba. The two facilities are open exclusively to the dwellers of Setagaya and Kawaba with quite reasonable rates.[52]

---

52 The two Setagaya facilities are built in the most interior section of the ravine in the village. Professor Odagiri at the University of Tokyo, formerly a faculty member of Takasaki City University of Economics in Gunma, makes the point that those locations are well chosen in terms of sustaining marginal communities in the village. Typically, in a Japanese mountain village, human settlement as a hamlet is developed along a river valley. In a typical depopulation pattern, once the most interior settlement has disappeared, then the next one is abandoned. In this chain reaction process the rest of the valley's hamlets fall, as in a domino effect. This is caused by a sort of psychological effect rather than economic reasons. Odagiri observes that Setagaya's facilities' location works effectively to save the most marginal settlement, and consequently the rest of them (Interview).

Setagaya resident stays in Kawaba are filled with various outdoor activities, including harvesting, hiking, fishing, and handcrafting. Vegetables harvested by the urban children are brought to their schools in Setagaya and served for their school lunches.

In the beginning, especially during the first six to seven years, there were many misunderstandings and miscommunications at the official level between the village and the city, and also between their citizens. Many Setagaya people considered themselves simply visitors or tourists and behaved badly, and this raised complaints among Kawaba farmers. In response, Setagaya officials visited each farmer in Kawaba to hear their complaints and to talk about solutions. Then Setagaya officials in charge of the exchange program gave Kawaba visitors a lecture in advance of their stay, in order to have them fully understand the exchange program. A Setagaya official for the Kawaba programs, Machida, says,

"It takes a long time [to understand each other]. But it's not very long from a long-term point of view."

Setagaya, with a population of 800,000 is 200 times larger than the Village of Kawaba, thus there is a potential for a large benefit from this program for the Kawaba economy.

"The gross agricultural product of Kawaba is 1.6 billion yen (approximately US$ 11 million) per year, and this means that this could be sustained if only 10% of Setagaya citizens would purchase their agricultural commodities from the village with at least 200 yen (US$ 140) per year" (M. Miyauchi, Interview).

Kawaba products are occasionally sold in some Setagaya stores. Both communities have invited the other for their annual festivals. And Kawaba people benefit both economically and non-economically through face-to-face communications.

"We need no other partner than Setagaya. But we of course welcome anyone who visits Kawaba" (M. Miyauchi, Interview).

It is a remarkable comment that all Setagaya children share the same Kawaba experience, and that this practice has lasted for more than 20 years. This signals a happy union between two communities—rural Kawaba and urban Setagaya.

Setagaya and Mayor Ohba

Since his inauguration in 1975, Mayor Ohba of Setagaya, who had served in the municipal government as an employee for 30 years, has been known for his innovative policies and planning methods. The urban/rural exchange program was one of seven main components of the first ten-year plan of Setagaya, established in 1978. Prior to the formulation of this plan, the city office spent about five years, with a deliberation council organized by Setagaya-resident experts and professionals, surveying the needs of the residents. The ten-year plan covers policies for the next ten years, but it is revised every fifth year, taking into consideration changing social, economic, and political environments and residents' needs.

Ohba's approach emphasizes communications with/among local people and a sort of workshop in communication (Machida, Interview). Apart from their routine jobs in sections/divisions of the city office, city officials are organized as community communicators or facilitators. The city is divided into five administrative districts, and each of them has a number of residential and retailers' community organizations. It is an obligation of city officials to maintain communication with those areas for which they are responsible, and to facilitate discussions and communications among the residents and with the city office. The ideas and voices gained from these communications are incorporated in the ten-year plan and other policies. This approach to policy making affects, to some extent, the long-lasting and manifold development of the Kawaba/Setagaya exchange.

Selling directly to urban people

Kawaba farmers and people have enjoyed economic benefits from the exchange activities. Geoffrey Wiggin, Agricultural Attache to the US Embassy in Tokyo, who visited Kawaba in the 1980s, observes:

"One clear and simple example is in the formation of new and inexpensive marketing systems for agricultural commodities. These commodities can move from the village to the final consumer through the informal marketing network to get a more attractive price for the goods" (Wiggin 1985: 254).

According to Miyauchi's explanation, farmers in Kawaba seek an alternative to the market for selling their products. Diversity is one of the essential elements in the promotion of agriculture in Kawaba. Kawaba agriculture is one of "small quantities and diversified items." This may be the only way in which it will survive.

Apple farmers in Kawaba are selling the most expensive apples in Japan—probably in the world. They are sold locally or through mail order. Kawaba apple growers maintain close and frequent communication with their customers, many of whom visit them in the village. Some even keep as many as 6,000 customers in Setagaya on their computer mailing lists. Such close contact means that their customers know who produces their apples and even from which trees their apples come!

In 1985, nine farmers in the Nakano hamlet, the most undeveloped district of the village, organized an agricultural processing corporation, called Nakano-Nosan Co., Ltd., to produce juice, jam, and other specialized foods. Their products are sold locally and in some shops in Setagaya. The corporation itself does not seek a profit; rather it buys materials from the member farmers at the best price. In order to sustain this marginal hamlet through agricultural promotion without marketing systems, the farmers have reclaimed and invested in apple orchards, and strawberry and blueberry farms.[53]

'The Forest of Friendship'

In 1993, it was decided that an 80ha *Yuko no Mori* (the Forest of Friendship) should be established in Kawaba. Both municipalities are obliged to maintain Kawaba's forest. Originally projects were undertaken, on a voluntary basis by members of Kawaba's foresters and by students at Tokyo University of Agriculture in Setagaya. Cooperative activities of school children (from elementary to high schools) in Setagaya include planting, weed clearing, thinning, and mushroom culture. It is expected that through this program urban children will be given a chance to develop an awareness of nature.

A failed ski area project: Political clashes between pro-developers and anti-developers

After Nagai retired as mayor, he was replaced by Kobayashi, who served as mayor for just one term until he was defeated by a Nagai follower in 1987. Kobayashi

—with his supporters, including real estate agencies who welcome large development projects—planned to promote mass development projects by attracting private development capital. Consequently, a ski resort development was planned and finally completed in 1989 with a private developer's investment. The aim was to attract tourists in winter when there are few Setagaya visitors. Visitors to Kawaba did increase dramatically for several years after 1989. For example, there were 455,000 visitors in 1990, compared with 123,000 in 1988 (Kono 1994: 42).

---

53 Employees of the Nakano Nosan Co, Ltd., whom I interviewed said they are proud of the quality and taste of their products, and that it is impossible to compete against major food industries in price within the market system. For example, a small bottle of strawberry jam is sold for around US$3.50, while the same product can be sold at US$1.50 at a supermarket in Tokyo.

This was the time of what we called the Bubble Economy in Japan—the mid 1980s to the early 1990s. The price of land was jumping in an unprecedented manner, which attracted mass investment in the land by capitalists. Together with government policy that promoted resort development by utilizing private investors, rural land was regarded merely as a source of profit from mass development. When the bubble broke, the company bankrupted, and a debt has been left on the village office as co-developer. Moreover, the current economic depression has dramatically decreased the number of skiers to Kawaba. According to an anti-development community leader, Kobayashi planned to make eleven golf courses in Kawaba (Mitsuo Miyata, Farmer, Interview), all of which were canceled after his defeat by the current mayor.

Miyauchi admits that the policy initiated by Nagai and promoted by his follower, Yokosaka, has not been fully successful in gathering support by the absolute majority of villagers. Rather, in reality, probably half the villagers do not support it, or at least have little interest. During the last mayoral election in 1987,[54] when Yokosaka was elected for the first time, he had an 8-vote majority over Kobayashi. This was a hot contest with a more than 90% voting rate. This political opposition is not related to political parties; rather it comes from long-standing traditional factions maintained within the village community,[55] as well as being related to the degree of benefit from current village policies.

Resisting development and urbanization?

There were three major waves of the development and urbanization/ suburbanization boom that were counter to preserving Kawba's rural identity. The first was around the early 1970s when the Japanese economy was still enjoying a golden age of rapid growth. National regional development policy was symbolized by the doctrine of re-engineering Japanese islands ('*Nihon-retto-kizo-ron*'), as announced by then Prime Minister Tanaka in 1973. This policy aimed at introducing mass development on—and industrial relocations to—Japanese islands, while, at the same time, constructing infrastructure and networks of *Shinkansen* and freeways elsewhere. One of the community leaders in Kawaba recalls,

---

54 In Japan, a municipal mayor is elected every four years. In Kawaba, there was no opposing candidate for the 1991 and 1995 elections, and no voting was held.

55 A 33 year-old farmer who is a member of the anti-Yokosaka (current mayor) group explains that it is not mainly because of pure political debates, but rather because of highly emotional opposition between the two major factions in Kawaba (Tetsuo Seki, Interview). Also, he and some other villagers admit that not all villagers can enjoy the benefits from Setagaya, and those who don't have little or no interest in the current programs.

"The mid-1960s - 1970s was the big business boom. There were a lot of offers to build golf courses—leisure parks from developers—in our district (hamlet). Our ku-cho (representative of residential district/community organization) at that time, who is the mayor now, rejected all such offers. More than 80% of people supported his decision" (Mitsuo Miyata, Farmer/founder of a community-operated food plant, Interview).

The second wave was the so-called Bubble Economy in the 1980s. The price of land was jumping in an unprecedented manner, which attracted mass investment in the land. In rural areas this took the form of resort development with ski areas, golf courses, big hotels, etc.) by capitalists and private developers. Together with the then national government's policy on promoting resort development utilizing private investors, rural land was regarded merely as a place to invest for mass development. Miyauchi says they learned from their mistakes and have decided to focus exclusively on cultivating a firm relationship with Setagaya.

The third was the wave of suburbanization from Numata city. This is still going on today. Like many other Japanese cities which seem to be following the example of U.S. cities, Numata's suburbs are extensive and sprawling with malls, discount shops, and housing development, while its downtown community is becoming less active year by year.

Overall, with the exception of the failed experience with the ski resort, as its planners proudly emphasize, Kawaba (with initiatives of Nagai and his follower) has rejected policies that use a commercial-based mass development approach. The village is enjoying a rare phenomenon in the North Gunma region: a growing total population, a stable population of young villagers, and a large influx of temporary residents each year from the cities.

7.3. Evaluation from a people's perspective

"Demographic decline has stopped. Desirably, for Kawaba's development, we won't need more population. We've reached an appropriate scale of population" (Tokoji Kadowaki, Moved from Setagaya, Retired from the National Defense Agency, Interview).

Until the mid-1970s, just like other Gunma villages, Kawaba had been a village of sericulture and farming. Kawaba's population decreased after World War II, until 1975. Its major industries (sericulture and farming) also declined. However, during the last two decades, Kawaba has been gradually recovering. Its recovery is due, at least in part, to the promotion of tourism and the Setagaya-Kawaba programs.[56] Today Kawaba attracts close to 0.5

---

56 The recent increase in population appearing in the 1995 census is attributable to

million visitors per year. Its population has been stable, an essential factor in assuring the vitality of any locality.

The suburbanization of an adjacent municipality along R120 just reaches the Kawaba village entrance. Not only village officials, but also the majority of people I interviewed seem to desire that Kawaba maintain its rural landscape and identity. In this Kawaba has been successful.

How has the village done this? How does this unique rural-urban partnership program work for it? In the following, I will examine information gained from interviews, and present my response and opinion regarding the reasons for this success as well as the future direction of Kawaba.

An ideal partner for the union

I realize Setagaya is an exceptional partner in a positive sense for Kawaba, not only because it is a large city with a significant upper class population, but also because its government possesses good skills and expertise in many aspects of planning and policy implementation.

Regardless of a top-down way of planning and implementation in both Setagaya and Kawaba offices, assuring mutual gain should be important for the success (at least, success in sustaining and expanding the exchange activities) of the partnership programs. In this respect, and, more generally, in terms of overall economic development, how does the relationship affect Kawaba? Is it a successful partnership?

My answer is yes, and I consider this program the single most significant factor that has directed Kawaba's economic development and preserved its rural identity. Although I am not able to provide detailed statistical evidence of this (which is not the aim of this study), I would like to note some of the direct and indirect benefits of this partnership.

"Roughly speaking, out of (Kawaba's) 900 households, about 200 to 300 have some sort of involvement in the exchange programs (with Setagaya). As for farmers, probably 150 to 200 farm households do" (Akihiko Miyauchi, Manager, Setagaya-Kawaba Furusato Corporation, Interview).

Here Miyauchi is referring only to the exchange programs with Setagaya. If we look at the whole tourism and related sector, more people Would be involved.[57] Without a doubt, the unique partnership relation with the biggest

---

the opening of a home for the aging in the village which accommodates about 300 people, according to a village official (Miniru Miyauchi). Regardless of this fact, Kawaba's population trend has at least become stable. Statistics indicate this is not due to an increase in births, but rather to an increase in immigrants from outside Kawaba, particularly after 1988 (Kawaba-mura 1995: 7).

57 For example, about 40 people are employed in skiing-related services. More than 20

and probably wealthiest urban municipality in Tokyo impacts Kawaba's development in many ways, although these benefits are not distributed to all villagers.

Those who most directly benefit from Setagaya are farmers, especially those producing and selling apples and blueberries to Setagaya residents:

"I ship directly to my customers mainly by home delivery. ...It's a desirable advantage that we can set the prices ourselves. I see the exchange programs just as business" (Masayuki Kobayashi, Farmer, Interview).

"When you target Setagaya exclusively for your business, there are a lot of opportunities. For example, I'm doing ownership of apple trees. We sell an ownership 10,000 - 15,000 yens (approximately around $100) a year. I now have 2,000 owners. I ship my products to Setagaya's community organizations by home delivery service ...An average farmer maintains 1,000 such customers, here" (Mitsuo Miyata, Farmer, Interview).[58]

Kawaba's retail community is less active than it might be because of suburbanization/urbanization in Numata city, but it would probably have been more severely impacted by the growth of big stores in neighboring urban areas if it had not benefited from the exchange program and from village-led tourism development as a whole.

"A significant part of our customers are tourists. I benefit from tourism. Having more floating population (tourists) means our village is well-off" (Kazue Hyodo (Ms.), Convenience store owner, Interview).

"As for the actual exchange activities, frankly speaking, I think villagers, except children, want to keep it away. It's a one-sided love from Setagaya. ...I don't see any particular problem in my business. They left money with us. Local retailers organize themselves as a union, or sort of cooperative, that sells goods wholesale to village's tourist-related sectors such as hotels, skiing facilities, and Setagaya's accommodation units, to share (economic benefit from tourism), and I'm a representative of the liquor division" (Nobuyoki Seki, Liquor shop owner, Interview).

---

farm-inns appeared after the village ski area opened (Nakajima 1992). In addition, the Setagaya-Kawaba Corporation, a government-funded agency that implements and promotes exchange activities and programs, employs 40 staff, of whom 24 are from Kawaba (Akihiko Miyauchi, Interview).

58 Miyata also talked about his district, Nakano, which is, in his words, the leading farming community in Kawaba. This community does not have the problem of a lack of people who are in farming or of an aging farm population.

A housewife who acquired a tourism-related job recently said,

"The merit (of tourism) is job opportunity for housewives at the skiing facility, Denen Plaza (tourist center with gift shops, a dining facility, and some attractions), and restaurants" (Shimako Kobayashi, Kawaba Historical Museum, Interview).

Apart from material economic benefits, few interviewees mention non-material, i.e., spiritual benefits from the exchange program with Setagaya. This is, however, mentioned frequently by officials in both Setagaya and Kawaba. In addition, some interviews point to another non-measurable benefit to Kawaba, namely volunteerism.

Setagaya is well-known for active voluntary citizen activities, and is a Mecca of voluntary organizations. Takeuchi, a musical physiologist, who was once a Setagaya-based community activist involved in voluntary activities for local development, such as conducting child welfare programs, moved to Kawaba eleven years ago. He says the Setagaya office and its staff are exceptionally well-trained and have good skills in communicating and encouraging Setagaya citizen participation in various aspects of local development policy. In addition, Setagaya works with various professional experts and/or authorities in planning as advisory members, and utilizes their expertise. Both Takeuchi and Akihiko Miyauchi understand that such "know-how" is beneficial to Kawaba. Village officials' capabilities are improved by learning from Setagaya. A.Mihauchi confesses that most ideas concerning Setagaya-Kawaba projects, including planning of both events/activities and physical design of particular facilities, always come from Setagaya—its government and advisory members, including professors of planning and of agriculture.

"It's always been Setagaya-led, truly. We are fortunate that the Setagaya government is capable. We're lucky to have a good partner" (Akihiko Miyauhi, Interview).

He believes the main reason that the partnership activities have lasted more than two decades is Setagaya's capability:

"They associate with us reasonably and never ask too much. ...For example, they never request country housing development projects (for private use)."

Setagaya consistently appropriates an annual budget of 350 million yens (approximately $30 million) for maintaining the Setagaya-Kawaba Furusasto Corporation, an organizational entity for promoting exchange activities and programs. According to A.Mihauchi, Kawaba's biggest asset is a partner that is always seriously committed to maintaining good relations and preserving Kawaba's rural environment:

"Kawaba can be active, because Setagaya is always seriously involved. They have a critical sense that Kawaba's rural environment is a major asset to be preserved. ...We have been taught by them and have realized that we have a great asset: our land" (Minoru Miyauchi, Planning Division, Village office, Interview).

A financial commitment is essential in order that all programs and activities, whether for development or preservation, last. For this reason, and because of its commitment to preserving Kawaba's rural environment, Setagaya, which is perhaps one of the wealthiest municipalities in Japan, is an ideal partner for Kawaba.

Different views from people with no relation to Setagaya

As the village official emphasized, regardless of huge differences in population and financial means between the village and township, the two municipalities are assured equal rights in the exchange programs, along with a sense of mutual respect (M. Miyauchi, Interview). However, some offer a different view. They admit not all villagers benefit equally from the partnership with Setagaya and/or tourism as a whole,

"I know there's no support by the absolute majority for the exchange programs with Setagaya, as the results of elections tell. ...Not everyone can enjoy the merits from Setagaya" (Minoru Miyauchi, Setagaya-Kawaba Corporation, Interview).

Although I interviewed only a small number of people, at least my interviewees' views were highly supportive of preserving Kawaba's rural environment, and they generally had few complaints about the village's development, direction, and function.[59] Almost all interviewees are anxious about the current recession in the Japanese economy.

"I see a lessened critical sense of impending crisis not only among farmers, but in the community. It's a peaceful village, I am basically satisfied. It's a carefree place. ...I feel no inconvenience living here. And we can enjoy fresh air and clean water. I anticipate Kawaba will not grow or have its population fall dramatically. Contrary to general belief, Kawaba is essentially a wealthy village " (Eiji Mochizuki, Local bank clerk, Interview).[60]

---

59 It would not be appropriate to comment that there are no criticisms and complaints about the current policy and functioning of the village in my interviews. However, it is appropriate to add my impression that, compared with the response in the other five localities, Kawaba residents indicate a higher level of satisfaction with their development and preservation. Complaints tend to be minor and concerned with such things as physical design of facilities, ways of planning and organizing events, and anxiety over the current state of the Japanese economy.

60 Regardless of the bank clerk's view, statistics show Kawaba's annual per capita income is the lowest among the six localities I studied. However, his observation

"I love Kawaba because it's a peacefully quiet neighborhood, and there's a rural atmosphere that I like. It's a good small neighborhood where everybody knows each other. ...I don't want the village to become urbanized and developed" (Shizuka Miyauchi, High school student, Interview).

"I have observed our community hasn't developed any critical sense of the development, though it's an important thing to do, I believe, to mobilize the people as unified. It is probably because each individual is semi-well off, and they think it's OK, at least in our generation" (Tugio Endo, Kawaba Chambers of Commerce, Interview).

Although there is a limit to the current means of development that puts a heavy emphasis on relations with Setagaya and tourism, it is clear that people prefer safer and cleaner places to—live like current Kawaba—if jobs are assured in or around their village, although more generally this depends on an individual's values.

Better transportation access

The explanation given by officials for Kawaba's success is centered on its link with Setagaya. However, Kawaba's success is attributable not only to mayor Nagai's charisma and his initiatives in developing this unique partnership relation with Setagaya, but also to its location. Kawaba is conveniently located near urban areas that offer Kawaba's residents access to places to work, shop, and recreate. Numata and many other urban areas in southern Gunma, including Maebashi and Takasaki, are within commuting distance from Kawaba. For example, it is a 70-80 minute drive to Maeabshi, the capital of the prefecture, via ordinary roads. According to the 1990 National Census, 31.4% of Kawaba's working population commutes to jobs outside Kawaba.[61]

---

should not be ignored because of the insight he is likely to have as a result of his business communications with the entire northern area of Gunma served by his bank. Because in rural areas like Kawaba, for example, most families own at least a small plot of farmland and a paddy field for producing rice and vegetables for domestic consumption, that saves on expenditures for food. Statistically, they are not categorized as farmers, and such production does not appear in income statistics. The more subsistence farming a village has, the lower the per capita income that is required. My interpretation of his word, "wealthy," is not one that is measured by economic variables, but rather one that includes quality of life considerations.

61 Concerning this figure, Kawaba, compared with other localities in Tone County, to which both Kawaba and Niiharu belong, along with six other villages/towns, has the third-highest figure in the county. The same figure for the other five localities in this study is as follows: Nakanojo (24.8%), Niiharu (22.3%), Ueno (12.8%), Kurafuchi (29.5%), and Ohgo (52.9%). Since Sawada is a part of Nakanojo, no figure is available.

Of these, 68% have jobs in Numata. Takematsu, a migrant from Setagaya, observes,

"Kawaba has a good economic foundation. Agriculture is semi-active (because of tourism-friendly agriculture). Numata is close. We have Setagaya. ...Yet still, many local people haven't realized 'we're lucky.' If there were no relations with Setagaya, Kawaba would either be swallowed by urban sprawls or dying" (Narimitsu Takeyama, Interview).

Nevertheless, I do not consider that Kawaba will have no problem in continuing to retain and attract a younger population, especially those who are well educated. The reality in Kawaba will, in this regard, be the same as that in many other Gunma villages located in hilly and mountainous regions, although the degree of seriousness may be less in Kawaba compared to others investigated in this study.

7.4. Concluding remarks

For Kawaba's future, as well as its current functioning, I see an amenity village on the urban/rural border as an exceptional *place* in an unevenly changing geography of rural space of Gunma. My point here is that Kawaba is functioning at the moment as an amenity village on the border of an urban core, and I believe it can continue to function in this way in the future. But if it does, it will be an exceptional case in terms of the spatial theory that New Urban Economics teaches (see Chapter 1). According to this theory, in modern capitalism, villages and cities become integrated economically into one continuous "space," with cities functioning as the core of capital accumulation, and villages becoming part of the urban periphery. Kawaba's unique endowments, however, may allow it to retain its characteristics and identity as "place," rather than losing them through economic integration into urban space. Kawaba would, in this case, be an "exceptional fragment" in the geography of New Urban Economics Theory. I believe Kawaba will preserve its rural identity. Relative to residents of other communities I investigated for this study, interviewees in Kawaba indicated a high degree of satisfaction with living in the village. What is the basis for this satisfaction?

In my opinion, amenity is one of the major elements that makes people satisfied. Many residents referred to a healthy, safe, and peaceful living environment; a locational advantage related to shopping and commuting; and the beauty of the countryside. Almost all villagers I interviewed said that preserving rural identity and the farming landscape are the top priority issues for the future. This is not only in order to attract urban people to visit, but also for the amenity of the villagers.

In sum, following are the reasons that Kawaba has been successful in maintaining a stable economic and population base while preserving its rural landscape.

First of all, Kawaba is fortunate to have an exceptional partner in its unique urban-rural partnership. Setagaya (a) plays a remarkable role in preserving Kawaba's rural environment, (b) provides an economic and financial base, and (c) shares its expertise and ideas about planning and implementation of public policies and projects. This is a most exceptional situation in which the village residents (and their friends in Setagaya) can enjoy rural amenities as well as urban upper class perks. Setagaya's effects should be evaluated more from the aspect of its impact on preserving a rural landscape with a small but active farming community and protecting it from growing urbanization in adjacent localities, than from that of the distribution of economic benefits. If you were to drive along R120 and its branch from Numata to Kawaba, you would see land use patterns change dramatically before and after entering Kawaba. Visible urbanization and suburbanization (i.e., large supermarkets, neon signs, or fast food restaurants) end just before the Numata-Kawaba border. This is due to a difference in zoning under the Urban Planning Act. The Setagaya office, including its external advisors, has directly affected the view and philosophy of Kawaba's political leaders in terms of both physical design and land-use policy. It was the needs of Setagaya citizens that transformed Kawaba from an undeveloped mountain village of Gunma into an amenity village for urban people. In exchange for this transformation, direct economic benefits came to Kawaba in the form of business opportunities in tourism-friendly farming and employment in related sectors/facilities. Half the villagers support this partnership. And almost all villagers agree: Kawaba's rural identity should be preserved.

Second, there were distinctive initiatives and exceptional leadership by the charismatic mayor Nagai. It was his initiatives that opened the door to a unique urban/rural partnership—and tourism in general—in the late 1970s. In the absence of such a mayor at that time, more than likely the village would have invited mass development projects such as housing, golf courses, resort hotels, and/or large factories. In that case, it would have lost its rural identity. Subsequently, Nagai's strategy was enhanced by the construction of *Shinkansen* and the Kanetsu Expressway in the 1980s, both of which serve Numata city and offer dramatically improved access to Tokyo.

Finally, in my analytical observations based on interviews and document research, I can confirm, to some extent, that Kawaba's success is not due simply to the benefits brought by Setagaya and/or tourism as a whole. The advantage in location not only assures improved access for urban residents to the village, but it also assures Kawaba residents access to jobs outside the village. Could a remote village like Ueno, which will be investigated later in this study, successfully implement the same strategy as Kawaba? The answer is probably not.

CHAPTER 8
GUNMA'S COLONIAL WILLIAMSBURG: AN IDEAL RURAL RESORT?

8.1. Introduction

The village of Niiharu is located in the most northern area of Gunma Prefecture as a part of Tone County, where the Tone River originates. (The Tone is one of Japan's major rivers; it provides water to the Tokyo area.) A branch of the Tone, called Akaya River, runs through the village north to south. Niiharu's area is 182km². The land use pattern is as follows: forest/wilderness (84%), farmland (7%), housing (1%). The community is surrounded by 2,000-meter mountains. It is located 160km from Tokyo, 50km from Maebashi (the prefectural capital and largest city), and 13km from Numata (the nearest urban area). Today R17 runs through the village along the River Akaya. Despite Niiharu's unfavorable topography, its accessibility was dramatically improved during the 1980s with the opening of the Kanetsu Expressway and the *Shinkansen*, both of which run between Tokyo and Niigata via Tsukiyono township (a locality adjacent to Niiharu). Today Niiharu is only a two-hour drive from Tokyo.

The current municipality of Niiharu was established in 1908 as the result of two mergers of 12 villages in 1896 and 1908. The Niiharu area can be divided into twelve hamlets which basically represent the areas of the original villages (Arisue 1993: 5). The village developed and grew with the Mikuni

Street, which connects Edo (the former name of Tokyo) and Niigata, a city facing the Japan sea, and Sado island, in which major gold mines operated.

Niiharu has the advantage of being located around hot springs. Historically, Niiharu was—like other Gunma villages in the past—a village of sericulture and "*onsen*," meaning, in Japanese, a popular traditional resort. There are about sixty inns and hotels in four *onsen* spots in Niiharu. These *onsen* areas are located in the interior parts of the village along R17, which is a traditional travel route to Niigata; they are, thus, not adjacent to the core tourist attraction areas, *Takumi-no-sato* and farming areas, which form the basis of Niiharu's heavily promoted agritourism.

Today tourism represents the major portion of the economic base of the village. According to the 1995 National Census, 55% of the work population is engaged in the service industry, most of which is tourism-related. The rest are employed in manufacturing (29%) and agriculture (16%). About one fourth of the work population commutes to work outside Niiharu.

Niiharu's population has been decreasing. It decreased most severely during the period of Japan's rapid economic growth. For example, its peak was 10,300 in 1960, and today it is 8,177. 21% of the population is 65 or older. Recent census counts show that the population decline has slowed.

8.2. Description from a policy perspective

"The beautiful landscape of a rural village is created with well-preserved paddies, and farmlands with farmers and foresters that are part of the landscape. We wish this village to last forever as a place to which urban people can visit for touching, beautiful nature" (Pamphlet of the Village of Niiharu, translated by the author).

Today, Niiharu is famous as a model of rural revitalization through the promotion of rural tourism—or agritourism. This means that it successfully preserves its rural identity by creating an economic base that depends upon that identity. In the last two decades, the village office has promoted tourism; its success has added a new face to the rural resort village of Niiharu. Today, one million people come to the village annually, 0.4 million of them to visit the core attraction area called *Takumi-no-sato*. About 50% of the population is involved economically in tourism, including farmers, retailers, wives, and elderly citizens. In the following sections, I present an overview of the various projects, using explanations of policy planners.

The pilgrim trail, the beginning

Nane Abe, the chief of *furusato* development in the village of Niiharu, states,

"There was nothing but agriculture and onsen-tourism here. As sericulture declines, mulberry fields are abandoned. We were looking for something to do instead of sericulture" (Abe, Interview).

There are a number of small, old, stone Budda statues by the roads and streets within a radius of 350ha of a district of Niiharu called Sugawadaira, where other buildings of historic interest, such as old temples, houses, and towns, are preserved. In 1978, the village began promoting stone-Budda pilgrimages to attract tourists to this area. The idea was simply to have people walk along the village road and see the Buddas, just like old pilgrims. Since no capital investment was needed, this was a low risk idea for the local government, and it was successful in attracting tourists.

"The idea of a stone-Budda pilgrim trail was originally practiced in the Azumino region of Nagano Prefecture. We borrowed it from there. There were no particular individuals playing leadership roles regarding this project. It just came from discussions in the village office" (Interview).

The village official continues,

"The success of the pilgrim trail attracted other businesses. Visitors need a place to eat. Farmers can sell their fresh products locally. Mulberry fields were reborn as apple orchards and gardens for tomatoes, corn, grapes, and cherries. ...Through this experience, we acquired the confidence that we can make it."

The pilgrim trail now attracts thirty to forty thousand visitors to the village annually. However, this development was not without criticism. Many complaints were raised in the community due to the fact that visitors spent little money, and so the economic impact was small, and because farmers in the district regarded visitors on their farmland as a nuisance to farming (Mizoo 1996: 163).

"Takumi-no-sato," the craftsmen village

Village tourism, which had been centered on the pilgrim trail, entered a second phase in 1985. The village office solicited financial assistance from the Ministry of Home Affairs for the purpose of reproducing traditional houses in the area of Sugawadaira in which local handicraft artists could demonstrate and exhibit their work for tourists. A historical museum of the Sugawadaira community and a farmers' market were added. By 1992, other traditional houses had been renovated with financial assistance from the national ministry and prefectural government and added as tourism attractions. This renovated, old rural community was given the name of *"Takumi-no-sato,"* meaning the craftsmen's village. As *"Takumi-no-sato"* became well-known, the number of visitors grew, reaching 0.4 million a year today.

Mizoo, a tourism development expert, who has been involved with Niiharu's tourism development ever since its beginning with the pilgrim trail, maintains that tourism has a number of positive effects upon the village: 1) it creates income opportunities, especially for the elderly; 2) it plays a central role in the cultural promotion of Niiharu; 3) it promotes local agriculture through marketing farm products to tourists; 4) it creates the basis for the village park plan, which will be described later in the section; and 5) it creates tourism-related businesses, such as farmers' inns, shops, tea rooms, and restaurants, thus supporting the revitalization of the Sugawadaira community. (Mizoo 1996: 163).

The success of *"Takumi-no-sato"* is accompanied by a change of landscape: abandoned mulberry fields become   orchards and vegetable gardens and are used to support tourism.

The "rural village park" plan

The success of *"Takumi-no-sato"* brought positive changes within the village, but its benefits were concentrated mostly in and around the Sugawadaira community; they were not spread evenly throughout the entire village. This raised criticism from the rest of the village. To address this criticism, the village office introduced the village park plan as its top policy priority.

In 1988, a project team for planning the further promotion of tourism and agriculture was formed. It was Mizoo (professor of tourism at St.Paul's University, Tokyo) who advocated the "rural village park" idea, in which a park is not a bounded area, but, rather, the entire village territory. People come to enjoy the historical heritage and landscapes, the local culture, and nature. The essential concept is that of linking agriculture and tourism for village development. A successful connection between tourism and agriculture will not only bring benefits to both sectors, but it will have spillover effects on other sectors, such as village commerce. In 1992, the Niiharu Rural Village Park Corporation (hereafter NRVPC), a non-profit foundation funded by the village office as an institutional arrangement, was established to promote various projects relating to this plan.

In this plan, *"Takumi-no-sato,"* meaning villages of craftsmanship, is one of the core zones for this project. The area is 300ha and includes four hamlets. In 1990, the village office implemented a municipal ordinance on landscape preservation, which regulates architecture in the traditional village and prevents inappropriate building styles.[62] Seven other core zones are to be

---

62 According to Abe, the village official who lives in the Takumi-no-sato area, the incident that triggered this action was a conflict between a new immigrant and old residents. A new resident in the Takumi-no-sato area from an urban area—a lecturer at the University of Saitama—built a modern house for his residence, which was obviously inappropriate for the landscape there. In addition to his unusual speech and actions,

created by utilizing existing resources, including a lake created by dams, a ski area, and *onsen*. In addition, new tourist attractions, such as a village-owned orchard park and a newly built *onsen* public bath, called *"Yushinkan"* will be created in order to distribute the economic benefits of tourism to other parts of the village. The aim is to distribute benefits from investment in tourism in a more equal manner throughout the village. *Yushinkan*, the public *onsen* center with a dining facility, is located in the hamlet called Irisugawa, which is the most remote part. It will help to provide jobs for aged and female workers in the community.

Just as in other rural municipalities in Gunma, during the time of the Bubble Economy there were many offers for commercial-based mass resort development projects in Niiharu. Abe proudly says, *"we rejected all such offers from private developers"* in order to keep the rural environment of the village as the asset which attracts people (Abe, Interview).[63]

The Furusato Fund

In 1993, the village office established a fund called *Niiharu-mura Furusato Kasseika Kikinn* (Furusato Fund), meaning a fund for the revitalization of Niiharu village. The fund—with a capital grant of 50 million yen[64]—provides for various expenditures, in order to preserve the native architectural style of individual houses in Niiharu and to promote community-based self-development efforts.

New job opportunities for farmers, wives, and the elderly

Efforts to promote rural tourism provide farmers with further opportunities for promoting agriculture and related activities. Niiharu agriculture has operated on a small scale and produced diversified items; it has never been large-scale, mono-cultural agriculture. Farmers have shifted from the conventional way of selling though the market to direct sales to visitors, which is much more profitable.

The village office has played a key role in promoting agricultural production. For example, it distributes free soybean and buckwheat seeds and buys soybeans and buckwheat back from farmers at fixed prices. At the processing plant of NRVPC, the soybeans and buckwheat are processed into *miso* and *saba* noodles, both of which are essential to the Japanese diet. The

---

which raised ill feeling among neighboring communities, this made village people consider some sort of regulations (Abe, Interview).

63 Various laws, including the Agricultural Land Act and the Forest Act, have been enacted that prevent the conversion of agricultural or forest land to other uses, such as commercial or resort developments, without government consent.

64 Approximately, US$0.35 millions.

Niiharu Center for Utilizing Aged Labor,[65] through which elderly people in the village can find jobs in farming and agricultural processing, was established within NRVPC. Also, local women, presumably mostly farmers' wives, organized in order to learn and practice agricultural processing and to create additional businesses. (Abe, Interview).

Growth in agribusiness opportunities has resulted in increased disparity in income among farmers. According to Abe, some devoted farmers earn more than 1000 million yen (US$0.7 millions) in a year. However, at the same time, others are still not doing well or have become worse-off (Abe, Interview).

An industrial park project

In 1988, under the initiative of the village office, 20ha of farmland were converted to an industrial park zone. An automobile plant and R&D center of a trans-national corporation (TNC), called the Aichi Corporation, were invited to Niiharu, in order to create local employment opportunities for young people. The automobile plant produces and exports special-purpose vehicles—such as truck-mounted aerial lift platforms for construction use. According to the general manager of the plant, out of 350 employees at Niiharu, 250 are local, which means Niiharu villagers comprise 71% of the factory's labor. One third of the R&D staff is also recruited from villagers. Out of 60 R&D staff, 20 are Niiharu-born engineers with degrees from universities in the cities (Toshikazu Mori, Interview).

The manager recalls,

"We were looking for a place where young labor and a large factory site were available. So far we've had no problem with this location. We have another plant in Ageo city, Saitama Prefecture; so we needed to find a convenient place from Ageo, in terms of transportation for our new plant. If the Kanetsu Expressway were not available to Niiharu, we wouldn't have chosen this location. ...One of our board members is from Gunma, and he knew Niiharu wanted to attract factories. Their only conditions were the factory buildings' color and they were looking for a type of industry without water pollution. ...At that time there was no industry in the village" (Interview).

Mayor Suzuki and Professor Mizoo

Two key individuals have played significant roles in the planning and promotion of current policy. Kazuo Suzuki, who has been mayor since 1988

---

65 Suzuki is advocating his "pension plus 600 thousand yen" plan. He explains that the elderly can make additional earnings from hobby farming or newly created jobs if the village park project is successful (Suzuki 1998: 14-15).

and who was formerly the chair of the village assembly, promoted the concept of the rural village park plan.[66] As mayor and politician, he told me of his dream for the Village-Park project--that it be a vehicle for promoting and preserving the village through the creation of a new economic base connecting tourism and agriculture.

"Our starting point is different from the others. When our effort began it was a time when people simply saw rural villages and agriculture as no use, out-of-date. ...It is important that our people become proud of their village being rural. ...You know, 80% of urban people are originally from rural villages. That's what makes our tourism possible. It's not simply tourism but education. ...Today, our society is facing a problem with children's minds going downhill. Experiencing our rural culture must be a necessary education for today's children. ...In terms of job creation and making profit, we will make further development. We've already created jobs for women and the elderly. It gives them a clear will and motivation to do something. Inviting urban people is important in this sense. Then with more people coming, more economic demand is created. ...For this purpose, it's important how we make our village beautiful. So, villagers' awareness is critical. This is the only way for a small mountain village, like ours, to survive. ...If the beautiful village, in a true sense, can be achieved, our village will enjoy development" (Suzuki, Interview).

Suzuki proudly maintains his rural-centric view, captured in his statement that the 21st Century will be a time for villages. He emphasizes the value of rural areas, including nature, environment, culture, and history, and is a proponent of a new paradigm for rural development that has emerged since the end of the Bubble Economy in the 1980s, in which rural values are central to development efforts. Suzuki believes that there is a favorable wind for rural and farming communities (Suzuki 1998: 12).

Suzuki emphasizes that his proposal is different from development based on conventional tourism, which merely earns money from visitors. Rather, his essential aim is to promote farming in areas that are unfavorable to large-scale agricultural production. This is, in his view, the essential element in the economic base, and it is also the key to being "rural."

---

66 One of his supporters maintains that Suzuki was the first democratically elected assemblyman to have a clear vision and will. In his explanation, despite political democratization after World War II, local politicians had never been democratic leaders in a true sense. Rather, the assembly was viewed as an honorary post for the elderly. Hence, assemblymen never developed sound political views or skills. Suzuki was first elected to the assembly at the age of 27 with an election promise of introducing cable broadcasting (Hyashi, Local businessman, Interview).

Professor Yoshitaka Mizoo of St.Paul's University, who is an expert on tourism development, has long been closely associated with Suzuki. He advised Suzuki on policy planning since the time when he was a tourism consultant and Suzuki was an assemblyman. Mizoo values highly Suzuki's qualifications as a local political leader. He observed that mayors prior to Suzuki were puppet-like in that they had no clear political view, or that they only worked toward feeding particular businesses that supported them, and that they never considered the whole picture of village development. Now Mizoo serves as a member of a board of official advisors to the village; however, it seems that his deep commitment stems not from this official appointment, but more likely from his close friendship with Suzuki.

It was Mizoo who advised Suzuki and the villagers not to adopt the more conventional mass-tourism development path during the time of the Bubble Economy in the 1980s and early 1990s. And it was Mizoo who encouraged farmers who had suffered from the decline in agriculture to link tourism and agriculture, both of which are the basic components of the current village park plan (Mizoo 1994: 156).

Mizoo, who sees himself as a general practitioner for Niiharu, suggests that the role of external professionals in planning is critical, not only for the case of Niiharu, but elsewhere as well:

"See Kawaba? Most ideas come from professors and consultants, like Professor Suzuki,[67] *associated with Setagaya. In the case of Niiharu, frankly speaking, they come from me"* (Mizoo, Interview).

He sees Niiharu as a desirable place to build a resort. In a sense, he believes a resort,

"(By promoting agriculture) vitalizes the rural economy. And maintaining farming activity preserves the rural landscape, where urban people can enjoy a rich, rural resort life. This is essential to the village resort. Basically, if a lot of facilities and attractions are to be built in a village where agriculture is dying, it could not be a resort that local people desire" (Mizoo 1994: 157, translated by the author).

To what extent is Mizoo's vision realized? Can it be generalized to all villages in the 21st Century, as Suzuki says? What is happening within the village, and in which direction is it moving? The next section will deal with these questions mainly by examining the opinions of the people of Niiharu.

---

67 Professor emeritus of urban planning at Tokyo Institute of Technology. See the Kawaba section.

8.3. Evaluation from a people's perspective

Niiharu has successfully transformed itself from a poor, undeveloped village, based on sericulture (which has already disappeared), small farming, and *onsen*, to a village with an economy based on tourism—similar to a rural version of 'Colonial Williamsburg.' This transformation has been led by initiatives taken by village political leaders.

It is remarkable that Niiharu now attracts approximately one million visitors per year, especially since many mass resort areas in Japan have been severely damaged by the current recession. While conventional resort businesses (i.e., many resort hotels, skiing and golf resorts) have shut down and gone bankrupt, the number of tourists in *Takumi-no-sato* continues to grow.[68]

Tourism is the biggest industry in the village. And Mayor Suzuki's plan for the village tourism park creates a scenario in which all industries in the village—agriculture, commerce, handicrafts/manufacturing, and the *onsen* sector—will be interrelated and will share the benefits of urban tourism, which, in his view, would become the new economic base of the village (Suzuki, Interview). *Takumi-no-sato* is frequently referred to in travel magazines as one of the most attractive tourism spots in Japan. It is also referred to as one of the most successful cases of rural tourism in Japan.

In what follows, by using information gained from field interviews with villagers of various backgrounds, I will examine the extent to which Niiharu's development has been successful with respect to distributing benefits, and what makes its success possible in Niiharu.

Who gains? Who does not?

One noteworthy finding is that people's views on the current functioning and future direction of the village clearly differ according to where the people live and their occupation—in other words, according to the degree to which they benefit from the agritourism efforts led by the village office. Basically, the residential districts of the interviewees are: (1) the core area—in/around *Takumi-no-sato*—which draws a growing number of visitors; (2) *onsen* areas, where there are conventional *onsen* and related businesses (including inns, hotels, restaurants, and shops), and which are suffering severely from the current economy; and (3) the rest of the village, including the Irisugawa hamlet, where a new tourist-attraction has been built recently by the village office (*Yushinkan*—a public *onsen* center with a dining facility); and (4) the

---

68 At this point, the number of visitors to Niiharu's onsen spots is decreasing dramatically—just as it is in other conventional onsen resorts—because of the economic depression.

remaining of areas where nothing has happened regarding agritourism so far.

Those who directly benefit from the agritourism plan are farmers and retailers in and around the *Takumi-no-sato* area. Tourism brings some visible rewards for them. According to a village official, the most successful farmer in this area earns more than a hundred million yen per year (about US$0.8 million).[69]

"I moved here (from a more interior and hilly part of the village) five years ago. ...I'm lucky I could utilize tourism for my business. As I anticipated, my sales have doubled. ...In the future, I see, we will grow continuously, but it won't be so drastic. We've just started agritourism, and it's too early to say that it is firmly established here. Individual farmers should develop their ability in business and management" (Hiromitsu Kawai, Flower Farmer, Interview).

"I'm selling 100% for visitors (to Takumi-no-sato). What I'm doing is just producing apples and other produce, and selling it here. All Takumi-no-sato visitors come through my place. I'm just lucky with the location" (Sadayoshi Honda, Farmer with an orchard in the *Takumi-no-sato* area, Interview).

"I think we should promote this. I'd like to make a contribution to this community. ...My business is getting better because of tourism ...Farming here has hope. So, if Takumi-no-sato and farmers help each other, overall, our prospects are bright and encouraging" (Takeo Kenjo, Gardener, Interview).

"I don't think the direction to which the village is moving is backward. We have to catch the wave of the times. I know we're envied by people of other villages (because of the success of Takumi-no-sato). We're so-so OK. While other tourism spots are losing, you know, only Takumi-no-sato is growing. Even in Niiharu, the Sarugakyo onsen is having a hard time. At least, this Sugawa hamlet (the core district of *Taumi-no-sato*, including its main street) *is sort of vital, I think. ...Younger people aren't leaving so much as compared with other hamlets in the village"* (Ichiro Koike, Liquor shop owner, Interview).

---

69 Residents of communities in and around Takumi-no-sato are not of one mind with respect to the desirability of promoting agritourism and preserving historical village landscapes. For example, in the Sugawa hamlet, through which Takumii-no-sato's main street runs, and where the majority of residents are office and factory workers, residents do not welcome having their neighborhood busy with tourists, and some are unhappy with old-fashioned housing. Retail shop keepers and farmers, however, generally support the preservation of traditional architecture (including individual houses) and welcome tourists.

A local bank clerk's observation supports these comments and the view that Niiharu's economy is, at least, better than that of neighboring localities:

"Of course, under the current depressed economy, the village economy is not very good. But my impression is that Niiharu is the most vital village in the Tone-Numata region (the Tone County and Numata City). *The Niiharu branch is doing the best business among our sixteen branches. Deposits are stable, and loans are not bad"* (Hiroshi Kigure, Local bank clerk, Interview).

In contrast to those who are well-off, people in the *onsen* and related businesses respond quite differently. Their complaints have mainly to do the current recession. Some are pessimistic about the future direction of their community and about their business. Others see Mayor Suzuki's village park plan as offering hope for the future. Villagers in the Sarugakyo district, which is the biggest *onsen* community in Niiharu, are critical of village policy.

To me, a buraku (hamlet) *always comes first before Niiharu as a whole. I can't imagine the whole village as one community. The basic unit is a buraku. Sarugakyo* (his *buraku*) *is economically de-vitalized. I don't think this is simply because of the influence of the current bad economy. Also, I see it (economic decline) as a long-term trend. The golden time was around 1960. We should've considered how to manage during a recession before. ...It's going to be economically difficult, so I am really worried about the future of this community. It's a sense of crisis* (Yasuyuki Tamura, Owner of *onsen* public bath, Interview).

"At least regarding (onsen) tourism, we fell off. It's visible that we have fewer guests. Also, I see we're going down as a whole village" (Shinichi Hayashi, *Onsen* inn owner, Interview).

"I have seen no influence from agritourism. There's no instant effect from Takumi-no-sato. I will never be well-off because of Takumi-no-sato. I have no interest in it. ...But, while the onsen community is declining, Niiharu as a whole may not be the same. Farming is moving toward a good direction. But (traditional) commerce is very difficult, while big supermarkets are growing" (Tahiro Fueki, Liquor shop owner, Interview).

"Onsen communities have just realized the real meaning (of what the village is promoting) ...We didn't have a critical sense, and we did have few interests in the village-park plan. Now our eyes have opened. ...We must consider things as a whole village. ...I welcome the current policy" (Takeshi Ishibashi, *Onsen* hotel owner/Village assemblyman, Interview).

Finally, villagers in other districts have diverse views on the current functioning and future direction of the village. In general, I observed that employed wage earners (office, factory workers) are optimistic with respect to the direction of the village, while self-employed people tended to be pessimistic.

"What the village is trying to do now is very good, I think. I'm happy that my village is well-known. ...I see our village is going in a progressive direction. It's a good thing to do, that we preserve the landscape, which is a wise way for local revitalization by utilizing the merits of the village" (Masaaki Koike, Working for NSK Co. (producing ball bearings), Interview).

"Our village is on the way for development. It's gradually getting better, if I compare life in 1970 to today. The biggest things are the Freeway and Shinkansen" (Masaaki Murakami, Mechanic for skiing lifts in Naeba, Niigata Prefecture, Interview).

"Earning workers have no problem. (Conventional) tourism is doing terribly, especially onsen. Retailers are doing poorly also. We are linked with each other. Big supermarkets are increasing. It's hard. ...We have to make up for the loss by inviting tourists. Even if our village struggles in some way, some who are growing will grow, some who are losing will lose. ...No one can escape from the competition principle. Our mayor can do nothing for that" (Yasunobu Hayashi, Owner of grocery stores and gift shops, Interview).

"The reason why I decided to begin dairy farming was because I thought this village would be less busy, with few people. I would not have needed to care about other people. I didn't expect such a busy village (with visitors)" (Kazutoshi Tamura, Dairy farmer, Interview).

Eguchi, a new resident who moved from Kawasaki city, Kanagawa Prefecture, came to the village two years ago. In the city he an independent engineer who, for more than twenty years, designed automobile production machines for, for example, Nissan and Honda. He offers the following as interesting advantages that bear on the socio-economic functioning of the village: 1) its locational advantage for his business (direct home delivery services of fresh vegetables) and excellent tourism resources that attract people to the village and his place, even though he is located neither in/around the *Takumi-no-sato* nor *onsen* area; and 2) the sometimes hidden fact that villagers are not poor, but, rather, somewhat wealthy, although in a different way from urban residents, and in a way not captured by economic statistics:

"At first I felt I was coming from another country. In Kawasaki, I lived in an apartment where sixty families reside. ...I now believe this environment and scenery are the biggest assets to be preserved. I dream of owning my own tourism farm here. ...After moving in, I realized a great advantage in location. For example, I can send (my farming products) with the home delivery service at

the same rate to anywhere in the Kanto block (including such cities as Tokyo, Yokohama, and Kawasaki, because Niiharu is still a part of Kanto). It only takes one night. I knew this after coming here. Also, we are lucky to have onsen, Takumi-no-sato, a Shinkansen station (in an adjacent locality). I thought how lucky this place is" (Eguchi, Farmer, Interview).

He continues:

"I was wondering how villagers could afford three cars per family, which rarely happens in the city. I came to find that they are not so badly-off. They have enough money to afford things. I realize that in the community there is a system in which people earn not from a single income source, but from multiple ones.[70] *They are sharing the money spent and earned in the village. I see they are spiritually rich as well as materially. When I was in Kawasaki, I was seeing a visible gap between the rich and poor, such as a poor tiny apartment beside a big fancy residence. I see few gaps here. Income opportunities are being created to some extent by the public corporation (NRVPC). They are offering employment opportunity for an equalized distribution of wealth. Things are going fine by utilizing the merits of being a small village. There are no such people who are very poor in terms of the quality of life. It's envious. I don't think life here is inconvenient."*

While, on the one hand, I am doubtful regarding the extent to which this observation could be scientifically confirmed, on the other hand, I do view this comment as valuable information. That is to say, this observer, as an outsider/insider, sees the current functioning of the village under the rural-village-park plan, in the context of the particular situation in Niiharu, as a means for development.

In the next few sections, I present those factors that make this hilly and mountainous village exceptional and that contribute to success of this development.

---

70 Let me add to his point. As an example, imagine the following family: elderly parents, both of whom receive a pension, who are engaged in small-scale farming producing food for both domestic consumption (thereby reducing outlays for food) and for sale at the farmers' market (created as part of the village park plan); a son and daughter who work at a factory or in the public sector, and who help on the farm on week-ends; the son's wife, who does occasional work in tourism-related jobs in a dining facility or gift shop created by the village park plan, while also taking care of her children. Although individual incomes of the family members are likely to be significantly lower than those that could be earned in large cities like Tokyo and Yokohama, the family's expenditures for food will be lower, and it does not pay rent (which is surprisingly high in major urban areas in Japan). In terms of its standard of living, the village family's income may be sufficient for them to qualify as "well-off" in Niiharu.

Excellent tourism resources

Niiharu is blessed with excellent tourism resources, each of them a component of the rural-village park.

First, as the foundation for the village park, is the nostalgic and beautiful scenery of an old rural village in which active farming communities have been preserved as part of the scenery. These farming communities are in fairly good condition in some parts of the village (but not in the entire village territory), and are part of the attraction for urban residents. In Japan, or at least in the Kanto region, traditional rural scenery has a scarcity value. This is not necessarily because of the direct influence of urbanization, but, rather, because of modernization. Life style changes have significantly altered the faces of towns and villages, through changes in the style of housing and shops, and the proliferation of signboards—all sometimes in an undesirable or haphazard manner. In addition, the mountains contribute to Niiharu's scenic advantage. I heard a village official say this about a visitor's comment:

"Visitors feel that Niiharu has the best balanced distance and inclination of the mountains as background scenery which makes viewers feel comfortable. While in other localities in this study such as Ueno, Kawaba, or Sawada, one may feel the mountains are too close and some may feel they are oppressive" (Yukio Abe, Interview).

Of course, beauty is a subjective value. Nevertheless, my observation, based on intensive field visits, supports the view that, among the six localities in this study, the countryside is best preserved in Niiharu.

Second, Niiharu has the advantage of having been a traditional *onsen* tourist resort. Although other localities also have *onsen*, they may be very small or have been built only recently as a part of *mura-okoshi*. Only in Niiharu and Sawada have *onsen* resorts achieved a certain scale and quality. Although Niiharu's *onsen* is suffering from the current economy, it will play a role in the rural-village plan when the recession ends. However, as Mayor Suzuki believes, the *onsen* community must make an effort to become more attractive.

Third, there are other tourist attractions, such as golf courses and a lake formed by a dam, in the village.

A convenient location

Needless to say, a convenient, accessible location is important for successful development based on tourism. In this sense, Japan may be different from, for example, Western Europe. Mizoo, an expert in tourism development, who has given advice to the village and mayor both officially and informally, points out an important difference in vacation travel between Western Europe and Japan. This difference relates to the ideal distance and travel time between urban areas and destinations. He maintains that, in many Western European countries, longer summer vacations, such as two- or three-week holidays, are common, but, in Japan, no such long holidays are established—even during the summer. In Japan, short vacations, such as a one-night trip on the weekend, are more common. This works in Niiharu's favor, as it is easily reached from the Tokyo area, using either the Kanetsu Expressway or the *Shinkansen* (Mizoo, Interview).

Human resources for policy planning

"After having the current mayor, village policy has visibly changed. He sees things from a long-term point of view. I didn't see this will in the previous mayor. He was the kind of person who only took the safe road. The current mayor's leadership is remarkable" (Masaaki Koike, Company worker, Interview).

I would also point to good human resources, including both leadership and expertise, as an important factor in explaining Niiharu's success. By "good" leadership, I mean good at initiating, planning, and mobilizing resources to implement policy. However, as Mizoo himself admits, the planning process in Niiharu has been highly top-down (Mizoo 1996, p.171). In fact, one of the interviewees (who supports another political group opposing the current mayor), while he does not entirely deny the aim and basic idea of the village park plan and while he values some of its benefits, observed:

"Everything is decided by some particular people: the upper strata of the village office (the mayor and a few officials) and their brains, by which I mean supporters (for the mayor) in each hamlet, assemblymen, and Professor Mizoo (Advisor to the village office and mayor)" (Shinichi Hayashi, *Onsen* inn owner, Interview).

Mayor Suzuki is not like the charismatic leaders in Sawada and Kawaba; rather he is the kind of leader who has good ability in managing and coordinating and who utilizes the expertise of others (Mizoo, Interview). Mizoo comments as follows on the effectiveness of the traditional top-down mentality of Japanese political leaders:

"In Japan, democracy is not the same as that in Western countries. It's always something where a (particular) person leads the rest (of the community). Then the local bureaucrats and residents are trained (by following him or learning from what he did), and human resources are developed. This is quicker at particular stages. There's no such sense of the citizen in Japan, while Westerners develop a more mature sense of the citizen as an independent individual" (Interview).

A detailed analysis and discussion of the quality of leadership is beyond the scope of this study. To summarize, the point that is important here is that a strong, distinctive political initiative by a local leader(s) is an important factor contributing to successful development.

Multiple bases for development

I have listed those factors, most of which are uniquely available in Niiharu, that I consider to be necessary to the success of agritourism in Niiharu. Are they all that is required for the continued success of this model? My answer is "no." As we can see from the above narratives, we should expect that there is a limit to what agritourism can do as a new economic base for the village.

And so, I would like to offer a critical appraisal of this policy and offer views that, I believe, do not receive appropriate attention from Japanese scholars and journalists.[71] For example, if maintaining a sound population base, especially of a younger productive population, or if attaining an appropriate level of population is an important condition for development, that should be a goal of an economic development policy.[72] In order to continue to retain and/or attract young people to the village, it be necessary to develop industry as part of the economic base.

Regarding the introduction of industry to the village, the representative of the Niiharu Chamber of Commerce offers his view that it is the Aichi Corporation[73] that makes the best contribution to building a basis for economic development:

"If Aichi were not available here, we would be suffering a serious population decrease. That's the biggest factor. I'm sure its contribution is greater than Takumi-no-sato, realistically speaking" (Yusaburo Seki, Niiharu Chamber of Commerce, Interview).

Aichi's general manager offers the following view of rural development:

---

71 For example, Mizoo (1996).

72 Another recent policy that I would like to note, briefly, is village-provided public housing (75 apartment units accommodating 200 villagers in the lower areas of Niiharu—the most convenient location for commuting to Numata and its train station). The purpose is to assist the relatively young, commuting population, and thus to promote the stabilization of a youthful population in Niiharu. In my interviews of residents who were not officials of the village, no one mentioned this policy.

73 A TNC that established a factory and brings some keiretsu companies to Niiharu's industrial park, and that employs nearly 300 young villagers. Refer to an earlier description in the section of the industrial park project.

"The important thing is a good balance of agriculture, tourism, and industry. It's just the same as diversification of company management. If a local economy depends on a single sector like onsen, it will fail when onsen declines. ...We're confident in being together with this village and its development" (Toshikazu Mori, General Manager of the Niiharu Plant, Aichi Corporation, Interview).

I agree with the opinion that economic diversification, is important. In this sense, Niiharu has been fortunate in that it has attracted other employment opportunities.

The limit of the current policy

Niiharu's population is still shrinking, but the rate is very moderate if we look at the last two census years (8,090 in 1990 and 7,925 in 1995). Nevertheless, almost everyone I met agrees that loss of the younger population is the biggest issue that hinders sound development of their community. They believe there is still a lack of good jobs for young people.[74] Mayor Suzuki holds that his village park plan contributes to creating new job opportunities within the village. Is that true, and is it enough? Some of my interviewees feel differently.

"I want to major in economics at a university somewhere in Tokyo. If there are attractive companies I would be interested in, I would be glad to come back here (to live and work)" (Takahiro Abe, High school student, Interview).

"As my son who left the village says, there are not enough jobs. ...My daughter left here too. There are not enough jobs for people with college education. ...There are only farming and tourism-related jobs here. Well, there are only kinds of jobs like working in gift shops, restaurants. Part-time labor is enough for that. Young people do not work in such places. In fact, there are not enough jobs in the winter because of fewer visitors. It would be ideal if there were a research center or something, so that young (educated) people could work in the village. Now, jobs are available only during the tourism seasons and the labor demand is limited" (Yoshisada Honda, Farmer, Interview).

"The essentials for development are companies, educational institutions, and other employment opportunities for the young. That's 'ichiban' (the best). Otherwise

---

74 The result of an opinion poll (N=597, randomly sampled) held by the village government (Niiharu-mura 1996, p.93) supports this opinion. In response to a question on the top priority policy issue, "expanded job opportunities" is given the top priority (29%), followed by "better environment" (26%), "improvement in medical/health services" (24%), and "improvement in transportation" (24%).

Niiharu's future will be difficult" (Yusaburo Seki, Niiharu Chamber of Commerce, Interview).

When I talked to Mayor Suzuki, I frankly asked him about this point. He did not respond with a clear answer. He emphasizes that employment opportunities for the aged and female labor have been generated by his agritourism plan, and he repeats that his plan should be expanded so that it will work for further economic revitalization of the village. Tourism, while it is the biggest industry in Niiharu, will not be enough.

Who resists?

Before presenting my concluding remarks, I would like to touch base with the people who are resisting, or are unhappy with the current functioning of the village.

Okada is a leader of the Niiharu Environment Group ("*Niiharu no shizen o mamoru kai*"), which has been resisting both a ski resort project that has been proposed by one of the major private developers in Japan and another dam project proposed by the government for the interior mountains of Niiharu at a site that is inhabited by golden eagles and two other species of eagles that are recognized by the Red Data Book as endangered. Okada states,

"The basic idea (of the village park plan) is understandable. But it lacks a commitment to serious ecological issues. The village and mountains are interconnected. Our village is linked, through sharing of the same river systems, with the Mikuni Mountains in back of the village. We should live together in the truest sense of the term. We see a lot of contradictions in the current projects promoted by the village. Farmland consolidation projects create damage to the ecology. They once planned to make a para-gliding field (on a hill by clearing forest) which was consequently canceled. That's a contradiction, isn't it? Niiharu is a place where different mountain systems meet, and, environmentally, topographically, it is blessed with a rich and unique ecological system. There are diverse vegetation systems within one village. It's a place that man shouldn't change. It's a place we shouldn't develop. Our living environment is based on that ecosystem. Some say, man or golden eagles, which is more important? That's nonsense. It's OK as far as the village operates Takumi-no-sato. But further development in the more interior regions shouldn't be allowed. ...We should conduct scientific research to define a desirable zoning of the core and buffer areas" (Yoichi Okada, Member of the environment group/*Onsen* inn owner, Interview).

His views on the future of Niiharu with respect to development differ from those of others:

111

"We should re-think it. What's development? Does it only mean money, income, or something? Is having a smaller and aging population a bad thing? Why? It's natural that young people do not stay in rural areas. If only Niiharu could keep young population... That's unnatural. Look around elsewhere in Japan. The same thing is going on (in rural areas). What we need to do is consider in what way we are going to live by considering such a reality" (Okada).

Okada's comments raise a fundamental question about development, especially rural development. Most of the villagers I interviewed want to retain the rural environment as part of their identity, but not out of a deep environmental concern. There are even a few who welcome more urbanization-like development,

"Environmental preservation requires less population. As the material culture has prospered, the environment has been negatively affected. Maybe it's good not to be developed. But I believe development must come first before the environment. We need more work places. That's the most important thing—big enterprises, manufactures, mass-tourism developers, like Showa village (another village in Gunma) where a factory of Canon has been recently built" (Hiroki Kigure, Local bank clerk, Interview).

Regardless of these criticisms, in a very general sense, people see some hope for the future in the current functioning of the village.

8.4. Concluding remarks

Niiharu leaders have successfully transformed a village of sericulture, forestry, and *onsen* into a successful agritourism village. As a result, *Takumi-no-sato* has become Gunma's 'Colonial Williamsburg'—a rural version of it. With financial assistance from state ministries and prefectural departments, Mayor Suzuki plans further investments in districts other than *Takumi-no-sato* in order to create further tourist attractions. This would bring to fulfillment his plan of a village-park over the entire area of Niiharu. This would, in his view, revitalize the community while preserving the beautiful and traditional scenery and an active farming community. That is, it would revitalize the economy while maintaining Niiharu's rural identity. Mayor Suzuki believes that this will provide a new economic basis and employment opportunities for this mountain village.

Can his plan meet the development needs of the village? My judgment is a qualified "Yes." However, this strategy may not be capable of generalization to other rural communities. There are four particular reasons for its success in Niiharu:

(1) *Excellent tourism resources*: Niiharu has diverse tourist-attractions;

(2) *Convenient location*: Improved transportation assures easy access for tourists;

(3) *Diversified economic base*: While tourism is the biggest industry in Niiharu, there are other components of its economic base both within the village and in neighboring localities (even though the existing base is not powerful enough to keep young people within the village); and finally

(4) *Human resources*: Vigorous leadership and good expertise for policy planning are available in the village.

How will the village function in relation to the changing geography surrounding this rural locality? If the village park plan is appropriately implemented and expanded (despite the warnings of environmentalists), it could result in an improved system for distributing more evenly throughout the village the wealth brought to the village from urban areas. But not everyone would reap the benefits. In this picture, Niiharu would function as a rural resort on the exterior fringe of the great metropolitan region of Tokyo, and it would maintain its rural identity. It would have do so in order to continue to attract urban people. However, in this scenario, the possibility of retaining or attracting younger productive people, regardless of the hopes of many villagers, would be limited.

CHAPTER 9
THE ROAD TO A GHOST VILLAGE, OR...?

9.1. Introduction

Tano County of Gunma is comprised of six municipalities. It is the most severely depopulated and economically the least desirable part of Gunma—and probably of eastern Japan,[75] despite its close proximity to Tokyo. The village of Ueno is located in the most interior part of the county. It has the lowest population density among 70 municipalities of Gunma.[76] As one of my interviewees in Sawada describes it, "It is Gunma's Tibet." Road improvements have rendered Ueno less remote. But still, in order to reach Ueno, you must drive 1.5 hours from the nearest freeway over a poor, partially one-lane road (R299), with steep ups and downs and bends along the gorges of the Kanna river.

Ueno consists of thirteen residential sub-districts, some of which are small hamlets. Major residential areas are located along the main road (R299), and some small hamlets are located along narrow gorges and cliffs. The latter communities are now disappearing due to an aging population. One may be surprised that such a village is located only 100km from Tokyo, the global city. In fact, among the six localities in this study, it is closest to Tokyo, as the crow flies.

The current village was officially created by the merger of seven original villages with the enactment of the modern municipality system in 1889.

---

75 With the exception of Hokkaido.
76 9 people per km², in 1995.

Hence, the area of present day Ueno is huge—182km^2. The area has a square-like shape, with each side being 15-16km. Forest covers 94% of the area, followed by farmland (1.5%) and residential use (0.2%).

Until the 1960s, Ueno had been highly self-sufficient, with only a small amount of interaction with the outside world. Just as in other Gunma villages, the major industries in Ueno had been sericulture, small-scale agriculture, and forestry—all of which are almost extinct today. The village's population reached its peak in 1955 with 4,854 people, but since then it has decreased to 1,586 in 1995, which means a loss of 65% of its population in the last four decades. This is the highest recorded depopulation rate among Gunma municipalities. One major difference in the population trend in Ueno compared with the three villages discussed earlier, is that in Ueno the population is still decreasing at a rapid rate—10-15% every five years,[77] while in the former villages either the depopulation rate has slowed significantly since the 1980s, or population has been increasing. Official figures show that 37% of the population in Ueno is 65 years or older; however, the actual figures is likely to be higher (estimated as more than 40%).[78]

Today Ueno is a village with no industry to provide a stable economic base. In addition, despite the recent improvements to R299 due to a dam construction project in the most interior part of Ueno, compared with villages in other regions of the prefecture, access to urban areas is inadequate. This hinders villagers from commuting to jobs in neighboring urban localities. The public sector, including the village office, fire stations, health/medical services, post offices, agricultural and foresters' cooperatives, offers the only stable employment opportunity. Employment in the public sector represents 40% of total employment (1995) in the village. A visitor to Ueno would observe a lot of ongoing construction projects—bridges, roads, tunnels. These projects are funded with government money. Retired farmers, who in their sixties or older, earn wages as construction workers. This is a common phenomenon in Japanese rural areas, but Ueno's case is probably among the more remarkable.[79] Statistics indicate agriculture and/or forestry sectors still

---

77 Except for the last half of the decade (1990-1995), due to construction of a hydroelectric power station which will be described later.

78 In Japan, a citizen must be registered in a family registry in the municipal office of the village, town, or city where he/she lives. In Ueno, many young people of senior high school age or older move to other regions in order to attend school. During this time they maintain their registration in Ueno. Thus, official statistics include a population which does not actually reside there.

79 This is now a large industry to sustain the livelihood of 40% of workers and their families.

represent 19% of total employment, but most of these workers are extremely small-scale,[80] self-sufficient farmers.

9.2. Description from a policy perspective

Of the villages in this study, Ueno has experienced the most severe social and economic decline. As in the cases discussed previously, political leaders of the village see tourism as the hope for Ueno's future. What pictures are being drawn in the planners' minds? What is actually going on in the village? To address these questions, in the following section I offer planners' narratives with my interpretations.

The "sixth" industry

"Tourism promotion and local industry development are our top-priority tasks" (Asakawa, Interview).

Ueno, or Tano County as a whole, unlike other villages in northern Gunma, does not have a history as a major resort area. Unlike other northern Gunma regions, Ueno does not have enough snowfall for skiing. Perhaps Ueno's resources for development based on tourism lie in its deep forests, gorges, cascades, and mountains. However, these resources are not unique to Ueno, as they are to be found elsewhere in mountainous regions of Japan. In addition, inconvenient access and unfavorable topography hinder the advance of mass tourism development. Despite these disadvantages, Ueno's local elites now see hope in promoting rural tourism. They use, as a keyword, "sixth" industry ("sixth" industry = "primary" + "secondary" + "tertiary" industries) to describe their concept of tourism as an organizing principle for village economic revitalization. This simply means that they propose the integration of the primary sector (agriculture, forestry/logging), secondary sector (food processing, woodcraft manufacturing), and tertiary sector (shops, restaurants, hotels, or direct marketing) for the promotion of tourism (the "sixth industry").

Neo-communism?: Expanding public sectors to feed the people

As mentioned above, construction projects and the public sector, both of which are funded by the government, are the two major 'industries' in Ueno. Under the leadership of Mayor Kurosawa, in the past three decades the village office has attempted to promote new businesses in manufacturing, agriculture, and tourism, in addition to building infrastructure. Early efforts

---

80 The average farm size in Ueno is only 0.3 ha, the smallest in Gunma.

were spent in the development and promotion of new agricultural products,[81] while recent efforts have gone toward building facilities for tourists. In 1978, the village office introduced a woodcraft industry, which is still being promoted. In recent years, using funding assistance from various sources, it has created a number of tourist attractions, built a number of facilities for use by the villagers, and engaged in the construction of basic infrastructure. Projects include a restaurant/giftshop (1980), a woodcraft showroom (1987), an apartment for the elderly (1988), a woodcraft training center (1989), a logging plant (1992), a day-care center (1993), a confectionery plant (1994), a tourist information center (1994), a Japanese toy museum (1995), a miso plant (1995), hotels (1967, 1995), and the "Ueno Sky-bridge" (a suspension bridge between mountains—a tourist-attraction, 1998).

These facilities are managed or operated by the village office or other public authorities, such as the Ueno Promotion Corporation or agricultural and foresters' cooperatives, with public money. These projects have created both temporary and permanent job opportunities for construction workers, the elderly, women, and some young people coming back and/or migrating from cities.

A village official provides an interesting view on the future role of local government:

"We think we need to expand job opportunities in such sectors (the public and related sectors) as much as possible to assure employment for the people. In this sense, our basic stance is different from that of urban policy makers. We have been playing a leading role, to some extent, in offering a work place. In my personal opinion, this village may possibly be a neo-communism-like community in the 21st Century. This would be a social experiment" (Ichikawa, Planning and finance chief, Village office, Interview).

Woodcrafting

In Ueno economic development policy, the woodcraft industry is given an important role. In his recent book, Mayor Takeo Kurosawa recalls,

"When I began to think about introducing other industry into the primary sector, I was interested in attracting factories to the village. In fact, once, one factory producing parts for the lighting industry came to Ueno, and also some other subcontracting factories, such as one for sewing, and began operations. Those factories could provide jobs for part-time labor, but never stable employment opportunities for sustaining one's livelihood. Three or four years later, once the bad economy took over, they reduced operations and finally went out of business. Such

---

81 For example, producing meat from a cross between boars and pigs, and mushrooms.

a business was not a reliable source for sustaining villagers' livelihood because of unstable management and low wage levels. Learning from this experience, I began to think that the desirable industry for dwellers' livelihood should be managed by ourselves with our capital. A well-suited manufacturer for a mountain village should be one that utilizes materials available here" (Kurosawa 1996: 204-205, translated by the author).

Today Ueno is well known for its high quality, handmade woodcrafts (furniture, table wares, toys, etc.), an industry that began just two decades ago as a result of Kurosawa's idea. The Ueno Foresters' Cooperative (hereafter, "UFC") and the village office have promoted employment opportunities in woodcrafts. About 60 people are engaged in woodcrafting, including 18 younger craftsmen who migrated with their families from cities after quitting urban jobs. Normally, those who have no experience in woodcrafting are trained and employed by UFC. Some successful craftsmen (ten, so far) are independent of UFC.

In the 1980s, Mayor Kurosawa wrote,

"Now (1985) Ueno's woodcraft, introduced in 1978, has grown nearly enough to reach our initial goal: a one hundred-million-yen industry.[82] ...There are people who have come to the land, having left villages and felt hopeless. We have welcomed two craftsmen from outside to the woodcraft center. ...Some become independent craftsmen. When the craftsmen village materializes because of such people, it will be time to say that our mura-okoshi has succeeded" (Kurosawa 1985: 75).

Ueno's woodcraft industry is now at a turning point. Sales have fallen off, partly due to a shrinking demand caused by the current recession and partly due to its weaker market competitiveness against other less expensive domestic and imported (from China, for example) wood products.

The Ueno Promotion Corporation

In 1998, the Ueno Promotion Corporation (hereafter, UPC) was established with a capital grant of 90 million yen (10.3 million for the first phase) from the village government. UPC is an organizational entity whose purpose is to undertake businesses and programs that will promote Ueno economically, while preserving it environmentally. The three core programs of UPC are 1) tourism promotion: managing and operating village-owned tourism facilities such as hotels, camp sites; 2) woodcrafts: establishing   woodcraft centers

---

82 About US$830,000. In recent years, a very rough estimate of the sales of the Ueno woodcraft industry has been in the range of two or three hundred million yen annually, according to Ichikawa (Interview).

(production) and showrooms (sales); and 3) forest preservation: maintaining Ueno's forests. Yukio Ogawa, the executive manager of UPC who was appointed by the Gunma Prefectural Government, presents this view of Ueno's potential:

"Access to Ueno is not easy. We've few people, and an aging populace is in progress. They see Ueno as a "backward" region. Yet, the times are changing. More attention from urban people goes to rural areas. So, we can attract people by promoting nature. We'll try to cultivate tourists who will visit us repeatedly. What we need to do is appeal to them with Ueno's charm. What we can do with the villagers is limited because this is a village with a small population and little stimuli from the outside. It's important to create a people's exchange here. What we'd like to do is not only manage facilities like hotels, but also offer ideas about how urban people can find the charm of Ueno. For example, a woodcraft event is going to be held here this summer. ...This July we will hire two new employees from cities. We want to secure good employees to attract more visitors. ...It's desirable that more people find Ueno's charm which would attract more new settlers. The new people will help the older people realize their hidden treasure. It's ideal if they can open the original villagers' eyes through such an interaction. ...I see a favorable wind for us in terms of the trend in tourism. I believe there will be a chance to expand our business under such a trend. To meet this, we want to secure good human resources in terms of quality and quantity" (Ogawa, Interview).

No exact figure on the number of annual visitors to Ueno is available. However, the number of visitors to Kawawa Nature Park,[83] has been 30-40,000 annually since 1984 (37,000 in 1998).

Mayor Kurosawa

Probably the most famous thing in Ueno is its mayor. Mayor Takeo Kurosawa has governed the village since 1965 and is currently chairman of the National Association of Villages and Towns (*Zenkoku chson kai*, a lobbyist organization of rural municipalities). Prior to being elected mayor, he was the president of the Ueno Agricultural Cooperative. Takahashi (1986: 73-74) describes the village situation when Kurosawa became mayor as follows:

"If we consider the origin of a village, there is a reason why people come to a place: they find a place for production there. It is natural that people leave that place when it no longer functions as a place for production. In the case of Ueno, I am not saying it lost all conditions for production; however, it lost them quite critically. 1965, the year Mr. Kurosawa became mayor, was one of the peak times

---

83 The core tourism spot in Ueno with camp sites, the Ueno Sky Bridge, and a limestone cave, managed by UPC.

of population flow from the village. Every year, 150 people left the village, while remaining villagers were stunned—150 out of 4,000. The new mayor's challenge is creating jobs that give hope for the future, because no one will reside in a place where no sustainable jobs are available" (translated by the author).

As we have seen in the previous three cases, vigorous leadership by a local political leader is one of the important elements in development efforts in rural villages. In the case of Ueno, most of the ideas and efforts described above are a result of Kurosawa's powerful initiatives. While many of the ordinary villagers I met highly appreciate his devotion to promoting Ueno, local elites described him as follows,

"He is now 85 years old. Everyone is worried about his successor. Since he has been mayor for more than 30 years, everyone accepts what he says. He is more senior than any assemblymen today. ...Most ideas come from him. He is most sensitive to global and domestic situations" (Asakawa, Planning and finance section, Village office, Interview).

"He has been doing his job with strong leadership. But, if he could manage staff more skillfully, things would be better. He has been mayor too long. There should be other capable people in the village office. He lacks the attitude of paying attention to such people's opinions. An autocratic boss has pros and cons. He has been a dictator. As an example for cons, he sometimes made mistakes by simply copying an idea that works fine in other places. Some failed projects were due to his poor preparation. He didn't care about feasibility. ...So far the village has not utilized external experts" (Murayama, Ueno chamber of commerce, Interview).

"It's a typical top-down method. Our job is how to implement what he orders. He says 'I always consider things 20 years into the future,' but he points out trivial things too. He establishes a perfunctory planning committee, but he decides the policy by himself. Then all we do is persuade the local people" (Ichikawa, Planning and finance chief, Village office, Interview)

Probably without Kurosawa's initiatives, development would not have occurred. Nevertheless, while leaders in previous cases (Kawaba and Niiharu) wisely employed the expertise of external professionals, in Ueno, Kurosawa apparently made little effort to do so.

The hydroelectric power station project

Regardless of massive socio-economic and demographic decline, this is considered a golden age for Ueno. The village government enjoys tremendous financial well-being due to a hydroelectric power station and dam project (the Kanna River Pumped Storage Power Station Scheme: hereafter KPSPS) located in the most interior part of Ueno. The project was begun five years ago by the Tokyo Electric Power Company (TEPCO). This project brings huge financial rewards from the Natural Resources and Energy Agency (NREA)—a division of the Ministry of International Trade and Industry (MITI)—as well as tax revenues from TEPCO. These revenues to the village are for a specified period, and will not last forever.

KPSPS, with an installed a capacity of 2,700MW, is planned to be one of the largest hydroelectric power stations in Asia. It is assumed that the project will be completed by 2011. Currently it brings 1,200 workers, such as TEPCO employees, engineers, and subcontractors, from the outside to Ueno. Although these people do not pay taxes to the village, they do bring money into the Ueno economy.[84] However, about half of the KPSPS workers will be evacuated with the completion of the first phase of the project in 2005, and no TEPCO employees (except 5 to 6 maintenance staff) will remain in Ueno after its completion, since the plant will be totally remote-controlled.

According to Ichikawa, the planning chief of the village office, the village received a total of 2.1 billion yen (about US$18 million) from TEPCO as a financial reward for locating the plant in Ueno. In addition, financial grants from NREA/MITI will total 2.4 billion yen (about US$20 million). The village office does not have freedom to use these grants from NREA/MITI at will. The grants can only be used for the purpose of constructing facilities and only with the permission of NREA/MITI. After the completion of the plant, Ueno will earn annual tax revenues on the electric generators until its value has depreciated. An estimated initial (maximum) tax income to the village for the first year is 3 billion yen (about US$25 billion).

KPSPS is creating an economic boom in Ueno today. Currently 50-60 villagers are temporarily employed for KPSPS/TEPCO as office workers, drivers, cleaners, and so forth. Road improvements and construction to the project site, now completed, employed 150 construction workers from the village at its peak a few years ago. KPSPS has created a huge demand for land for building offices and employee housing, converting relatively good farmland into office and housing areas. This has accelerated further a serious decline in Ueno's remaining farming community and represents a permanent loss of farm land in exchange for temporary earnings from rent and employment. The village is now planning tourism development around the new lake created by the dam.

---

84 These people have no family registration in Ueno village, so they have no obligation to pay taxes to Ueno. Officially they are not regarded as residents of the village.

Local leaders' views on the future

To summarize this section, I quote narratives of five local leaders relating their views on Ueno's future. Village officials and other local elites speak with some hope, emphasizing the need for further tourism promotion after the completion of the TEPCO project.

"What I was most anxious about before the dam project was the reaction after the temporary boom. Farmers are employed by the project. All employees will be fired when TEPCO evacuates. They won't be able to come back to farming. Farmland abandoned for two years needs more than five years to recover. We're now discussing how to utilize 8ha of land currently being used for TEPCO housing. ...Exchange (tourism) should be important after the TEPCO project. We need more visitors, tourists. Hence we made the bridge, hotel..." (Ichikawa, Planning and finance chief, Village office, Interview).

"Realistically speaking, the village will rapidly get smaller and smaller if we don't do anything. Yet, is it a good thing to increase population more and more? I think there should be an appropriate population scale in the village. It's good that this village has become busy. Of course I know we can't keep an appropriate level of population in the current way of doing things. ...My ideal vision (of Ueno) is (a village where) the appropriate level of population is maintained, nature is preserved, and local people can enjoy economic benefit from something which I haven't figured out yet. To meet this, people's morale should be raised, their awareness should be enlightened. We should consider what businesses can be successful here. What venture businesses can we start here? Tourism is a possibility. Tourism-related business can stimulate the local economy, although I'm not prepared to say exactly what that would be. Tourism, local industry, and agriculture are to be linked" (Ogawa, Executive manger, UPC, Interview).

A village assemblyman describes his view of the village as a village-park, an idea which seems to resemble a Niiharu initiative, as described earlier.

"If I consider the main industry of Ueno from now on, it will be offering nature for urban people's relaxation. I think the whole area of the village should be made into a park. Ueno's agriculture and industry have declined. There, the service industry for tourists would be the main income source. In so doing, it may positively work for agriculture and industry to some extent. In this picture, a school and village office are located in the park. Our development shouldn't hurt the environment. It should be a place for urban people's relaxation, with fresh air, water, and greenery. Then they will loosen their wallets (spend money) here. That's the only way to survive (for Ueno). Woodcraft manufacturing will be given a certain role in this picture. Transformation of people's ideas is needed, I

think. It's people, not the village government, who should undertake this business. They need a sense of management" (Taro Nakazawa, Assemblyman/Head of a woodworking plant, Interview).

He continues,

"I'm an optimist about the future of Ueno, regardless of a number of problems to be solved. Our revenue will grow dramatically. We should create job opportunities with this funding. There'll be a wonderful future for the village. We have to invest in this with cooperation between the public and people. Our tax income (from TEPCO's electric generators) will be cut off in 2035 (due to depreciation of the value of the plant). We should invest money in things that work for self support of villagers and revitalization of the village" (Nakazawa, Interview).

Nakazawa believes rural tourism should play that role. Would it work for Ueno like it does for Niiharu? Contrary to Nakazawa, another assemblyman expresses a pessimistic view on the possibilities of that sort of tourism:

"The most desired thing is income opportunity. This problem cannot be solved by ourselves. They say we can make money by advertising Ueno's nature for tourism. I don't think so. They say Ueno has a beautiful natural environment—it's Switzerland in Japan. No kidding! there are tons of beautiful places elsewhere in (rural) Japan. They're telling a big lie. In fact, the river has been polluted. Of course I desire to preserve this environment. Yet we cannot live on farming and forestry any longer. No successors in these livelihoods remain in the village. All the young people besides those in the public sector have left the village for cities. In the past two decades, Ueno has become a village of old men and old women. It would be ideal if tourism could grow and the difficulty in transportation access could be dramatically reduced. Yet, it's impossible to ask young people to stay with their parents within the village. I am very sad to say that Ueno is going to be a lonely place where only elderly people reside, realistically speaking" (Toshio Soma, Assemblyman (Retired from farming due to KPSPS/TEPCO. He is now employed by a security company for construction projects.) Interview).

Finally, Toshio Kurosawa, the president of Ueno Agricultural Cooperative, also views Ueno's agriculture and industry (in his words, a conventional way of production) as largely hopeless. He maintains that a place like Ueno cannot survive in the same arena where everyone is fighting by producing and selling goods. Hence, he believes that Ueno should undertake another social function:

"I see a village of tourism and welfare as the future function of Ueno. If a facility accommodating, say, 500 to 1,000 elderly people is built, lots of medical and health workers and their families will move into the village. It would work for

the revitalization of this village. In this picture, Ueno is a place where people can spend the rest of their life—a place for healing one's life. The cost is paid by their families, urban people. In this village, it's hard to live within a conventional way of production: for example, a factory makes goods and sells them for a profit. Rather, it's better to wisely be with an aging society which is what is happening. Fortunately we're not very far from Tokyo. It's not bad to offer our place to retired business warriors (workers). It's impossible to make young people stay here. Otherwise, the village will die. Now I'm drawing my idea as a plan for a welfare village. When it's finished, I'll talk to the mayor about my plan. Or, an advancement of information technology such as the internet and a cable television system may bring the possibility of new business here that transforms this backwards village into something better. If so, that would be great" (Toshio Kurosawa, President, Ueno Agricultural Cooperative, Interview).

In sum, local elites have all expressed concerns about both the current and future directions of Ueno; some see promoting tourism as the last (and only) hope.

9.3. Evaluation from a people's perspective

Despite the poor performance of Ueno's *mura-okoshi* efforts in terms of visible outcomes, the planning perspective is that at least Ueno has not been totally overwhelmed by the changing industrial, demographic, and economic situation. How do Ueno's citizens view this situation? In this section, I offer villagers' comments on the current state and future direction of Ueno.

Little influence from urbanization

There are no supermarkets, convenience stores, and big discount shops in the village. There are only traditional small shops and diners (restaurants). Despite the current economic depression, the retail community and small businesses in Ueno, such as shops and diners, are still active. In this respect, the situation in Ueno is quite different from that in villages studied previously. Continued activity is attributable to two major reasons: first, of course, KPSPS/TEPCO and its 1,000 workers create a huge market for local retail merchants; second, the remote location prevents competition from urban retailers.

Interviewees explain these factors as follows:

"There should be some influence of suburbanization, yet still it's not very visible here in Ueno. Many of them are only small shops and businesses operated by a family. The current situation is that they can still manage to feed their family. Since this village is located in an interior part of mountains, it takes 90 minutes to go to Fujioka (city). The elderly value traditional face-to-face communication

with merchants in their community. They still keep a sense of 'giri' (a traditional sense of moral obligation). Because both consumers and merchants are old, they keep such a relationship. ...Now, since people connected to TEPCO are staying in the village, we have more consumption. That hinders us from being influenced by the recession and supermarkets in cities" (Osamu Murayama, Ueno Chamber of Commerce, Interview).

"My business is relying on a face-to-face communication with the neighborhood. Most of my customers are elderly people who cannot drive or walk to go shopping by themselves. So, my main business is home delivery to such people. I am having extra sales due to the TEPCO project which probably represents 10% of the total. In terms of tourism, the village as a whole could benefit from it. But, to me, there'll be little benefit from it. ...After the TEPCO dam is finished, merchants will be suffering badly. We cannot make a business without people. The sales will drop. On the other hand, when a tunnel connecting Ueno and Shimonita township[85] is opened in the future, access to big shops in cities will be improved, and we won't be able to compete with them. ...So far we have been able to sustain our business because of poor transportation, while I wish for road improvement" (Kazuhisa Imai, Grocery shop owner, Interview).

"My sales are getting smaller as population declines. Yet, I have vending machines in TEPCO apartments, from which I earn 50% extra. In ten years, it won't pay enough with only local people. It's critical" (Seiji Sakurai, Grocery shop owner, Interview).

The future of the crafts' village

Some people express their skepticism about the viability of Ueno's woodcraft industry, which planners see as one of the means for creating further job opportunities and attracting new migrants from cities. For example,

"More than half of 1,600 villagers are in their forties or older. Ten years later, there'll be far fewer young people. A lot of people are currently engaged in construction work, but construction work won't last forever. We need a firm industrial base. Woodcrafts? In terms of the situation of the current Japanese economy, I'm doubtful that the demand for woodcrafts will grow. Maybe it can feed people currently engaged in it, but no further employment opportunity is expected from it. How many families can live as woodcrafters?" (Seiji Sakurai, Grocery shop owner, Interview).

---

85 Another rural municipality with a population of 12,000 also going through depopulation and aging. The Joshinetsu Expressway connecting Tokyo/Gunma and Nagano (newly opened in 1997) runs there.

Shuji Ohno is one of the most successful woodcraftsmen in Ueno. In 1988 he quit his office job in Chiba Prefecture and moved to Ueno with his wife and children. He has been an independent artist since 1991. Although he is not satisfied with the current direction of Ueno's woodcraft industry, in his insightful vision of the future for the village, he sees some hope in woodcrafts as, in his terms, an industry that can transmit new values or information from Ueno to the outside world.

"I'm worried about the future of Ueno's woodcraft industry. Ueno has been promoting it for 20 years. Nevertheless our outcome is still limited. It will be in decline, unless we make further efforts. What we're doing is just producing goods to sell to wholesalers who sell them to department stores. Our profit is meager. Ten craftsmen are independent. But most of them are merely subcontractors of UFC. They don't know the outside world. I'm guessing they could hardly live on such a wretched salary when their children grow. I can't imagine how much I will earn for our living. I don't know what's going to happen with the whole village either. ...My ideal is a computer-networking society enabling people to come back and live here again. I wish our woodcraft would attract new people. In the future, I hope people will be able to live in nature. Unless people come to the village, the local economy won't be stabilized. It's ideal that we have more population, industry, and more tourists. ...You know, people's values have changed. An individual seeks what he or she really wants. It's time an individual producer's originality was really demanded. ...A hardware of production such as a factory is not enough for the new industry. The important thing is software. The village should generate something new for the outside. The village should generate new information. It's ideal if people who seek such a value come to the village."

Although he uses the term, "new industry," vaguely, and he may refer primarily to woodcrafts, his comment is suggestive with respect to a future function for rural areas and rural industry.

Observations by new villagers

People who moved to Ueno from outside provided me with observations based on their previous experience. One person from a city talks about the difficulty of living in Ueno. Another, from another country, presents a philosophical view of the village's struggle for development.

Miyoko Sakurai is a nursery school teacher. She moved from Fujioka city, Gunma, with her husband, who quit his job in Takasaki and became a woodcraftsman in Ueno.

"The village office is very rich, but individuals are not. Income is unbelievably low. I realize, in Ueno, when a child becomes high school age, he or she has

126

to live in an apartment in a city, that gives an extra economic difficulty to the parents. They have to cut down on living expenses. I feel villagers develop a greater interest in their children's education, probably because of the poor life here. To educate children, they endure a poor life. The village built new facilities every year. But look at individual people. They're only construction workers. They work themselves to the bone. They have really poor wages. ...Now our income is one third that of when my husband and I were in the city. I'm surprised at the aging here. Officially it is said 32-33% of the people are senior citizens (65 or above), and it'll be more than 40% in 10 years. We should pay more attention to the elderly. They're still engaged in physical labor. When either of a married couple passes away, he or she has to live with his (her) son or daughter in a city or move into an elderly people's apartment. (So there are) lots of vacant houses. ...I'm renting such a house. In my community (Nippa hamlet), the neighborhood is all vacant. Some communities are disappearing. You know, some guys married to international brides (from the Philippines and Thailand) who don't speak Japanese. I teach them Japanese on a voluntary basis" (Sakurai, Interview).

Paul Emely from Wellington, New Zealand, taught English to children in Ueno for two years. He views the current and future situation in Ueno as follows,

"Now Ueno seems to be well-off because of the dam project. Now it is at a peak. Five years later, it's going to decline to what it was before the dam project. There are a lot of new facilities and buildings, compared with Nakzato (village) or Manba (township) (in the same county). The direction in which Ueno is going now is urban, but it's temporary. (After the dam is done) it will return to underdevelopment. New Zealand villages are the same, but Ueno has much more money. A dam makes money and good opportunity. It's a golden period now. But, young people leave. In New Zealand, this is also the same. Young people do not want to be farmers. They leave for cities. It's impossible to stop it. You can't make people stay who don't want to. No opportunities for good jobs are here. Now the Japanese economy is not good. There is no way to promote industry. It's a tourist-craft village. The same things happen in New Zealand villages, handicrafts, wineries... Actually, weekends are busy with tourists. It's only good for weekends, but not during winter. ...I feel sorry about this losing battle for which they are trying to build tourist attractions (with dam money). ...It's going to be a ghost village, (in which there are) lots of facilities but no people (Emely, Interview).

Pessimistic views of the future

Can tourism and a woodcraft industry save Ueno? Can they reverse the direction in which Ueno seems to be going? Can people envision what the village will look like thirty years from now? In a general sense, the village residents share the same anxieties expressed by policy planners; some feel it is impossible to alter the current direction of the village, Japan, and the global economy;[86] others express a strong desire for a breakthrough, although what that is, they do not yet know. An inn owner tells of his skepticism about tourism development and admits his business relies on the TEPCO project:

"Realistically speaking, I think there'll only be a few people here in 30 years. You won't see a young man often in the village. There used to be 48 families 30 years ago in this Nogurisawa hamlet. Now there are 27 families. Since there are no eligible women in the village,[87] some marry women brought from the Philippines or Thailand. There are probably at least six such international marriages in Ueno. When our community (Nogurisawa) was active, there was a branch school in the hamlet. The future looks so difficult. I'm quite pessimistic about it. ...Today our guests are mostly people from the construction project. We have few sightseeing tourists. ...This is not good for us. The village-owned campsite also has few tourists" (Tekehisa Kurosawa, Inn owner, Interview).

The massive decrease in population along with the aging of the population are the biggest and most pressing issues, based on my conversations with villagers. The majority of those I met feel it would be fruitless to plan changes in the village economy, given the broader context of economic and social trends. Some interviewees comment,

"My ideal village is a place where busy urban people enjoy themselves and relax, just like Grindelwald in Switzerland, as the mayor says. ...Yet, in reality this is a village where only old people live. Depopulation will bring the community to an end (Toshihide Fuse, Junior high school teacher, Interview).

"It's going to be a village of old people. ...Some communities (hamlets) will disappear. People in the interior communities buy a house and move to Fijioka

---

86 Among eleven respondents to my inquiry about future directions, nine people give a pessimistic view, while two are optimists. One sees her hope in tourism and the other expects transportation improvement with roads and tunnels to transform the village into a bedroom community for urban regions of the prefecture.

87 As a phenomena generally found in the Japanese rural areas, loss of young population is more serious with women than with men. Traditionally, it has long been considered that a family is succeeded by the first son and his wife. Hence the son is expected to stay in his village. To some extent, this custom is still observed in rural areas. On the other hand, it is generally considered that, since women have not the social obligations and traditional rigid customary practices found in rural areas, young women tend to leave for cities.

(city). Population decline will be the end. I'm very sad" (Tomie Tsuchiya, Housewife, Interview).

"Population will decrease dramatically. Few babies are born here. Thirty years ago, every family used to have children, when people were engaged in sericulture ...It's desirable if the village would have more people. It's impossible, I know. It's still good that people come back here from the cities after retirement. That's the direction the village is taking. This will be a place where people spend their last days" (Fumi Soma (Ms), Tourist information center, Interview).

"We have to find a way out of the present situation while TEPCO is still here. ...If it's difficult to develop industry, a good road that enables people to commute is needed. ...It's not bad to be a bedroom community. It would be ideal if we could have industry in addition to a bedroom community function. Anyway, realistically, Ueno will disappear unless something is done. What the village currently is doing doesn't work for it at all" (Seiji Sakurai, Grocery shop owner, Interview).

To be fair, I must note that not all people I met feel that the future of their community is hopeless. An insightful woman expressed her strong awareness of the need for action and for mobilizing people:

"We are being and will be affected by globalization which could transform the state of Japan. So, what we can do by ourselves is limited. A people-driven village is desirable, but Ueno is likely to be merged with other neighboring localities merely as one of the (backward) regions. To arrive at the ideal village, nothing will begin unless we take some action. It's not someone's business. It's WE who should be considering what to do. We all, each one of us, must work on this" (Keiko Iide (Ms), Health/Medical advisor, Interview).

We have now a gap between planners' expectations with respect to future village development and what the villagers feel, see, and think. This gap is a result partly of the villagers' ignorance—or distrust—of local policy, but it also comes from their objective appraisal based on their experience of daily life and business in the village. They all feel something is needed in addition to what the village is doing, but they do not know what that should be.

9.4. Concluding remarks

To create an economic base and additional employment opportunities, the village government is intensively investing in tourist attraction facilities. It considers tourism and a woodcraft industry to be the top priorities for its survival. Can this reverse Ueno's situation?

Unfortunately, I share the skepticism raised by some of the villagers. They recognize the need for a stronger, more diverse economic base if they are to prevent further loss of population, and if they are to attract new settlers from the city. At the same time, they wish to preserve Ueno's mountain countryside environment. This presents a big dilemma.

It appears that Ueno's elites are simply copying a rural tourism model similar to those that have been successfully implemented in Kawaba, Niiharu, and Sawada, even though Ueno does not share the same conditions and characteristics of these three successful cases. Unfortunately, Ueno's leaders are not aware of this reality. Can the village continue to prop up its economy by using government money to build facilities and infrastructure in the mountains? How long can the village continue to expand the public sector in a "neo-communism" manner?

From a realistic point of view, in the absence of an alternative development model (i.e. so long a the village continues to operate within the present planning paradigm), unless the village government effectively utilizes financial resources from NREA/MITI and TEPCO, or unless transportation is improved dramatically, I think Ueno will continue to decline both economically and demographically, and it will become a "ghost village."

CHAPTER 10
SUBURBANIZATION OR AN ECO-WELFARE VILLAGE?

10.1. Introduction

The village of Kurabuchi is located at the base of Mt. Haruna (1,449m); it is surrounded by 1,300 to 1,700-meter mountains. Among the villages we have examined so far, the village of Kurabuchi is closest to the prefectural economic and political center—the cities of Takasaki and Maebashi. (It is about 21km from Takasaki.) Due to this close proximity to urbanized areas, it could be expected that, compared with the four earlier villages, there would be both more jobs and a wider variety of jobs within easy commuting distance from the village, thus helping to maintain a stable population in Kurabuchi.

However, despite its proximity to Gunma's biggest urban areas, Kurabuchi is suffering a rapid decline in population; it is the only municipality in Gunma County presently experiencing population decline. Population reached a peak of 8,859 in 1950, but since then it has consistently declined until today. During the 1960s migration out of Kurabuchi to cities was intense. During the last three decades population has decreased at a rate of 4-6% every five years. According to the 1995 Census, Kurabuchi's population was 5,176, with 25% aged 65 years or older.

Just as in other villages, conventional small-scale agriculture in Kurabuchi is becoming weaker, and farmers, as well as other villagers, are aging. The exception is organic farms which are growing in number. In 1995, the percentage distribution of the working population by sector was as follows: 27% (agriculture including forestry), 35% (manufacturing/industry), and

38% (commerce and public services). The percentage of workers employed in farming in Kurabuchi is the highest among the six villages and townships in this study.[88] Out of 1,516 families[89] in the village, 808 (53%)[90] are farm households. Unlike other villages in this study, in Kurabuchi there are no major tourist attractions.

The current village was formed by the merger of two villages, Kurata and Toribuchi, in 1955. (Hence the name: "KURA-BUCHI.") Both of these originally consisted of smaller villages, which now function as residential sub-districts.

10.2. Description from both a policy and people's perspectives

In the following sections, I do not employ the format, used in the previous case studies, in which I compared planners' and citizens' evaluations. Rather, in order to describe what is happening in Kurabuchi, I offer, with my interpretations, views of both officials and the citizens on a number of topics. Kurabuchi differs in an important way from the previous villages (especially the first three): there is an absence of strong political leadership and clear strategic intent in its local economic development planning.

It is true that the village did take some development initiatives (most of which were not very successful in terms of visible outcomes), such as inviting factories to locate in Kurabuchi and implementing a plan to attract urban residents to Kurabuchi. Nevertheless, throughout my field interviews in Kurabuchi, I did not hear a clear policy statement or comments on the village's future direction from local bureaucrats and politicians. This may be due in part to the fact that the next comprehensive plan (for the years 2000-2010) of the village office has still not been completed. My interpretation, however, is that people I met, even local elites, are still struggling to find what they should do in response to the rapid changes in economic and social trends.

"The village of flowers and verdure"

The following is the basic development philosophy of the village office, as stated in the comprehensive plan for 1991-1999.

"Kurabuchi has long nourished and maintained its rural culture, including natural environment and historical tradition, based on farming and forestry. This is a valuable asset not only for villagers, but also for busy urban people who seek a place to rest. We promote new rural development with creative actions geared to the various contemporary issues of welfare, education, and environment,

---

88 Excluding Sawada, for which no official statistics are available.

89 In 1998.

90 In 1997.

through consideration of such policies as rural-urban relations and human resource development. To bring this to realization, we propose a concept of 'a hand-made village with flowers and verdure' (hana to midori no tezukuri mura)[91] *in which various people can get close to and live with flowers and verdure as the symbols of the village; people can cultivate mutual understandings and ties; and people can enjoy a rich civilized life and be well-off. To achieve this vision of the 'hand-made village with flowers and verdure' means creating a village within which people can feel pride and joy"* (Kurabuchi-mura 1991: 13; translated by the author).

To an outside observer, Kurabuchi is a quiet and beautiful place with flowers, trees, and rice paddies; in short, it presents a typical rural, Japanese landscape. People in the village, however—both elites and ordinary citizens—see and feel differently about their village and its future. Some say their village has little charm, and so there is little in which they can take pride, and little to attract outside people. Of twenty-five villagers I met, some say the situation is totally hopeless; others dream of an eco-welfare village. Almost everyone expressed uneasiness about the village economy and the loss of population. Some say development must come first; some say preservation must come first; others say both must be assured.

Groping for something in the dark?

Kurabuchi is just a very mediocre rural place in Japan, or at least in Gunma, in that there are no incredible tourist-attractions, industries, manufacturers, or major agricultural products. It is neither an isolated or remote place like Ueno, nor is it a traditional resort like Niiharu. Young villagers share a sense of ordinariness about their locality:

"I could find no answer to the question 'Is there anything (attractive) in your village?' Well, the only thing is maybe a delayed cherry blossom (because of altitude, so that urban people can come and enjoy the beauty of the trees). That's it. There's nothing attracting people here in terms of the whole community" (Noriko Omori (Ms.), Local bank employee, Interview).

"Our village will be better or worse, depending on policy from now on. ...The village's atmosphere is lifeless. The bad pattern is that it remains lifeless, and abandoned land is not effectively utilized. The village office once planned to

---

91 The Japanese language often tends to be ambiguous both grammatically and conceptually. A "hand-made village" is a direct translation from "tezukuri mura," the original Japanese words used by the village office. However, I, as a native Japanese speaker, do not understand the real meaning of the words. My guess is it is a metaphor in which a village is seen as a craftwork object, affectionately decorated with flowers and greens by villagers.

make a graveyard with the remainder of sand from construction of the Nagano Shinkansen Railways (running through neighboring towns, built in 1997). Fortunately, this has not borne fruit, but if it had, it would work for nothing in terms of attracting people (for vitalizing the community). You see, the village office lacks serious planning for the future. Unless we consider something to attract people, our village will remain just a deserted rural village" (Shoji Tsuchiya, Manager of a public mountain villa, Interview).

Nakazawa, a veteran village official, whose current appointment is agricultural and economic promotion, admits that—regardless of the basic development philosophy—there are no clear policy directions for economic development coming from Kurabuchi's local elites. They still have not developed a firm view about what the main issues and policy priorities are. He describes the current situation, in which they cannot discover a *mura-okoshi*, or village revitalization plan, as follows,

"We're still in a stage of trial and error (with respect to development planning). Shall we live with agriculture as the major economic basis? Or, shall we promote industrialization and attract corporations? We don't know" (Nakazawa, Interview).

He continues,

"Kurabuchi's population has decreased from 8,300 in 1955 to 5,200 presently. The agricultural population has been moving to cities. Earlier, the lack of transportation made access to cities difficult, so people did not have the choice of working in Maebashi or Takasaki unless they moved away from the village. Nowadays, even though access has improved to some extent, there are still few job opportunities in the village besides the two factories of Sanko Gosei (Ltd.) and Taiyo Yuden (Co., Ltd.), which employ nearly one hundred villagers. Young villagers desire to live in a city, at least for a little while. Once they move to a city, they rarely come back. Today it still takes one hour to commute to downtown Takasaki (because of poor roads and traffic jams). Other villages and townships in Gunma County are not in a mountainous location like us, overall. If you carefully examine the demographic trend of Gunma, Misato, or Haruna (other townships/ villages in Gunma County), for example, you will realize the fact that urban districts gain population while hilly rural districts lose. No suburbanization reaches here" (Nakazawa, Interview).

Regardless of this situation, political leaders of the village, including the mayor, assemblymen, and officials, have not drawn up a vision or plan for development.

The seamy side of development in Gunma

"Our community is moving in the direction of further decline. I've no hope for the future. This shop's going to be patronized by only the elderly. Village roads were busy before. The bypass road (the Jyoshinetsu Expressway) reduces traffic to less than half of what it was. Our sales have fallen by 30%" (Junko Hagiwara (Ms.), Convenience store owner, Interview).

As will be appreciated from three earlier case studies, modern forms of transportation—expressways and the *Shinkansen* train—bring tremendous possibilities for local economic revitalization to mountainous rural villages in Gunma. However, in the case of Kurabuchi, it works differently.

Historically, the village was located on a road connecting the cities of Gunma to major tourist resorts in Nagano Prefecture and other places in the more interior regions of Gunma (such as Karuizawa and Kusatsu—Japan's most popular resort areas). Kurabuchi's retail community, including shops and restaurants located along these roads, benefited from tourists driving through the village. However, the opening of a new expressway connecting Tokyo and Nagano (completed just before the 1998 Winter Olympic Games in Nagano), has dramatically reduced both traffic and local retail business, as a shop owner mentioned above.

Rural industrialization today

In general, the latter half of the rapid growth period of the Japanese economy was a time of rural industrialization—as capital searched the frontier for cheap labor and land for production (see Chapter 2). Branch plants of big corporations and their subcontracting factories were major providers of non-farming jobs in rural areas.

In Kurabuchi, in the 1970s. the village office made an effort to attract industry. As a consequence of that effort, today there are two factories of transnational corporations in the village: Taiyo Yuden, Co., Ltd , which produces electronics; and Sanko Gosei, Ltd., which produces machine parts, such as laser printer parts for Canon and Hewlett Packard.

Kennchi Urano, the general manager of Sanko Gosei's plant in Kurabuchi, explains that the reason for choosing Kurabuchi as a location for their new plant was they had customer companies in Maebashi and Nakanojo at the time (1973), and Kurabuchi was between the two places. Since Sanko Gosei no longer deals with the two customers in Gunma, their business has shifted from such local locations to international ones.

"We don't think that we will build other plants in domestic locations any more. We're expanding our international base of production. Our customers' locations

are globalized, so that we have to shift our production base globally" (Kennichi Urano, General manager of Kurabuchi plant, Sanko Gosei Ltd., Interview).

Kennichi Urano lists the pros and cons of having a production site in a domestic rural location like Kurabuchi:

"In general, an advantage of locating a plant in a rural area like Kurabuchi, is, first, that official support by a local government is available. Second, it costs less to build in a remote place compared to an urban location. The disadvantage (of a rural location) is transportation. This is not applicable to every rural location, but here (Kurabuchi) there is an inefficiency with respect to transportation. ...In the earlier days, we actively employed the local work force. In this sense, I believe we made a contribution to the local economy. But, as more automobiles are now in the village, young people tend to prefer working in cities. So, we have fewer applications from local people. What a company can contribute locally is employment opportunity. However, in a rural location we cannot satisfy our labor needs only with local employees" (Urano, Interview).

One of the characteristics of Japan's traditional and unique industrial structure is hierarchical integration of a parent company and its subcontracting firms. Generally, rural industrialization not only contributes to creating non-farm job opportunities in rural villages through large companies, but also through their subcontracting factories, most of which are small, family-operated businesses. But in the age of the global economy, as industrial production shifts from domestic to international locations, subcontractors in the villages lose their business. According to Urano, all orders from Sanko Gosei to subcontracting companies in Kurabuchi were canceled by 1998. He presents a pessimistic view on keeping remaining subcontractors in other locations in Gunma due to the changing business environment.

"We're the only subcontractor for Taiyo Yuden today. There used to be another one in Kurabuchi, but it went bankrupt. Also, there used to be some outside Kurabuchi. Taiyo has now made its production shift from Japan to foreign countries; it keeps only the R&D function at domestic locations. There are fewer remaining subcontractors like us. It's difficult." (Keiji Omori, Owner of a factory providing electronic parts for Taiyo Yuden Co., Ltd./Assemblyman, Interview).

As Keiji Omori mentions, globalization is removing part of the economic base from rural villages. Market liberalization of farm products, together with globalization of business, trade, and the market, are affecting the economic future of mountain villages in various ways—both directly and indirectly.

The Kurabuchi Kleingarten: A trial for village revitalization?

To implement the concept of the "hand-made village with flowers and verdure" in the comprehensive plan of 1991, there is a project that was introduced as a sort of symbolic trial. The Kurabuchi Kleingarten[92] was planned as a top priority project by the village office. The German term "kleingarten (little garden)"[93] is used to mean small garden plots that are rented to urban residents. The objectives of this project are stated as follows (Kurabuchi-mura 1997: 3; translated by the author):

> 1) to utilize abandoned village farmland;
> 2) to contribute to the benefit of urban people by providing the opportunity for relaxation through horticultural activities;
> 3) to revitalize Kurabuchi's agriculture and community through interaction with urban people; and
> 4) to promote an urban-rural exchange.[94]

Regardless of these official statements, in my understanding, the Kleingarten project should be viewed as a (*mura-okoshi*) business operated by the local government. It is essentially different from land allotment for community gardens, which in Germany are normally voluntarily operated by citizens or a community organization. In Kurabuchi the village office bought 4.2ha of abandoned farmland and built facilities such as a bungalow, a dining facility, and a gift shop, using financial assistance from higher governments, in addition to revenues from garden rentals.[95] The Kurabuchi Kleingarten was opened in 1991. A new *onsen* (hot spa) facility was added to it in 1996. Today sixteen villagers are employed by the facility, and several local farmers participate as tutors of horticulture. There are now 148 small garden renters, although this number has been decreasing.

The impact of this project is only very modest, both with respect to the initial objectives and in the broad picture of village development. The manager of the Kleingarten, who was transferred from the village office, admits,

"This facility was planned and begun in the peak of the (Japanese) Bubble Economy (the late 1980s). We intended to promote exchanges between villagers and urban

---

92 "Kleingarten" is pronounced as 'ku-ra-in-ga-ru-ten' in Japanese.

93 In Germany, under the Federal Kleingarten Act of 1983, kleingarten (managed by a city government or the federal railway) is given a certain role in urban planning as an open space and recreational place.

94 I suspect that Kurabuchi planners intended to establish urban-rural exchange programs much like the Setagaya-Kawaba programs.

95 Plots are rented for an annual fee.

visitors. However, I have to admit that we have to revise the initial aim . In the current recession, it's difficult to expect contractors to stay. At the beginning, we used to have more contractors from Tokyo. But we now have fewer people with renewed contracts. One reason for it is that similar facilities have begun to be found elsewhere. At least in Gunma, there are 70 similar ones today. It still takes at least three hours from Tokyo to get here. People prefer closer locations to enjoy horticulture. Therefore, we added an onsen facility in 1996. It's a very good one. Last year, cumulatively 115 thousand people came to our onsen.[96] Only 28% of those are from outside Kurabuchi. In terms of management, it's unavoidable that our business relies on profit from the onsen" (Norio Yamada, Manager, Interview).

From this, the following questions should be raised: What is the benefit to Kurabuchi created by the Kleingarten project, and who benefits? How has it worked in terms of economic and spiritual development of the Kurabuchi community? How many local people are participating in the exchange activity?

The manager explains that employment opportunities for villagers as well sales of goods, materials, and fuel by local merchants (annually 3.9 million yen) are the economic benefits of this project. But, in terms of the issues faced by the village, it is easy to conclude that the Kleingarten project makes little contribution, as village officials including the manager unwillingly admit. Perhaps the most significant—or only—contribution is that the village made a public bath facility which local people can use.

Absence of political leadership

In the earlier four cases, regardless of the performance and feasibility of their policies, we have observed visible policy initiatives by the local government (or SAC, in the case of Sawada) and clearly stated policy aims. In Kurabuchi these are largely absent. I see an absence of leadership, as some villagers have remarked:

"Unless a capable mayor would be available for us in the future, the most likely future of Kurabuchi will be a merger. Socio-economic decline will continue" (Keiji Omori, Assemblyman, Interview).

"I don't see any vision by our leaders, the mayor and village bureaucrats. What have they intended? So, our village will be reduced to half in terms of population in the future" (Yoshinobu Tsukakoshi, Company worker commuting to Maebashi, Interview).

---

96 Including villagers and those who come more than two times.

"Mayors, both current and previous ones, look like puppets pulled with strings by someone behind. And assemblymen like working for money. I don't see any positive energy in them that would make the village better. (They want to maintain) the status quo. Assemblymen are all old. They tend to allow no new ideas. Assemblymen are more powerful (than the mayor). There are two major groups opposing each other. They oppose everything" (Minako Harada (Ms.), Cook for the public school lunch center/housewife, Interview).

A horticultural therapist

The idea of a kleingarten was not introduced by the village elites; rather it came from a family that moved to the village in 1985. Nakazawa, the village official, recalls that the village was considering a policy for maximized land use in the village at a time when there was more abandoned farmland due to agricultural decline. Then a family came with an idea taken from Europe: community gardens. Nakazawa concedes that the village office's principal aim was maintenance of abandoned farmland by attracting urban people. It was neither a welfare nor employment policy.

Tatsuyoshi Kondo had lived in Germany for years as an employee for a trading company. He moved to the village with his wife and daughter to open a farm of horticultural therapy—a facility which provides rehabilitative therapy and vocational training to the mentally disabled through horticultural activities. He has also been involved, as an independent horticultural therapist/town planner, in a number of housing development projects related to the concept of a welfare town. His daughter, Manami Kondo, who studied horticultural science in Japan and Germany, is now a well-known garden designer.

Kondo developed his interest in horticultural therapy for mentally disabled persons when his family was in Germany.

"I have a son with a disability. Every parent who has such a child wishes for a society in which their child can lead a full life and live together with the community, don't they? That's an earnest hope. That's where we started. That's the way all parents like us think. I really appreciate having a son who gave me a valuable opportunity to associate with various people (with the same wish). I see by and large everyone has a sickness. Elderly people, the majority of the villagers, might have some problem with health. Some people have a disability with their hands. Our society consists of diverse people. Hence normalization (of the circumstance surrounding disabled people) is important. The term, barrier-free, is important not only regarding a physical facility but also regarding all environments. I believe a rural village is an ideal place for realizing such an environment. You see, those who engaged in agriculture are now all aged people.

I see this as a picture of what welfare should be. And we're now entering the aging society, you know" (Tatsuyoshi Kondo, Horticultural therapist, Interview).

Kondo sees Kurabuchi as an arena for the realization of his dream of a barrier-free society (for the disabled, the elderly, and everyone else). He considers his current activity to be the first trial for his dream. However, as he, as well as some other villagers I interviewed, admits, his attempt was not fully understood by the rest of community, and there is little communication between him and others in the community.

"We shouldn't consider future local development solely from the perspective of money values. Welfare, health, environment, and education are all equally important. Yet, in actual practice, it's difficult. People have long been trapped in old customs and ways of thinking in this village. They are extremely conservative. It's understandable that young people hate this place and leave for cities. An idea like mine never comes from this village. Probably villagers aren't understanding what we really see and mean to do, I suspect. They are utilitarian. They merely think that if people come from the outside it's good because they can rent the idle land. They didn't know 'kleingarten' is not for business" (Kondo, Interview).

He emphasizes the importance of networking and communication, which he and his business lack presently, for developing awareness in the community and for the transformation of the overall environment of the village, including the environment and people's attitudes. Despite some problems, Kurabuchi is attracting growing attention as a place known for horticultural therapy.

Organic farming, a growing sector

Another group of people that is active and growing in number consists of organic farmers producing cabbage, lettuce, and a variety of vegetables, fruits, and rice. In the latest decade, they have enjoyed growing—or at least stable—sales and incomes, despite the decline of conventional farming and of other sectors, such as manufacturing and services, in Kurabuchi. A growing awareness of food safety has created a huge demand for organically produced food in Japan, especially in the last one or two decades.

Yamada, a Kurabuchi-born farmer who began organic farming eight years ago says his sales grew 2.5 times in this period. He speaks of his hope for Kurabuchi's agriculture,

"I personally see that agriculture in Kurabuchi is not hopeless. Rather I have had a good response to my business for sure. I know the farming population in this village as a whole will be shrinking in terms of number. But it's OK. Agriculture should be undertaken by those who are enthusiastic." (Interview).

Kurabuchi's organic farming was introduced and promoted by one enthusiastic farmer, Mr. Sato, during the 1980s. In the latest decade, organic farming has been doing very well in Kurabuchi, which could now be considered a Mecca for organic farmers. Organic farmers are presently the most active people economically and spiritually in Kurabuchi. Mr. Sato is now playing a leading role in the organic farmers' group of Kurabuchi, and in Gunma as a whole. He and his group invite people with an interest in beginning farming to Kurabuchi, where they provide them with various kinds of assistance. Today, 25-26 families are engaged in organic farming in the village; half of them are relatively young migrants in their thirties or forties, who have quit their urban jobs. Yamada points out that the boom in organic farming in Kurabuchi is due in part to the advertising power of the Kleingarten.

Rejecting modernization?: *The eco-welfare village as a scenario for the future.*

Will the horticultural therapists and organic farmers be the movers and shakers in Kurabuchi? The information I obtained from interviews suggests that there has been little interaction between the new villagers and the rest of the village. In that case, what do the new people see as a scenario for the future of Kurabuchi? How do they wish to relate with the rest of the community? The horticultural therapist and organic farmers I met share the same values. Yamada, the organic farmer, emphasizes communal ties as an essential value. But there is no significant dialogue between this group and the rest of the community.

"It's the same everywhere—more aged people and fewer young people. Is it only a good thing to have young people? There should be some communities where older people gather. Is this a bad thing? Entering into the aging society, there'll be some ways of moving that we can take. In capitalism, things are going to be money-oriented, while it's going to be difficult to help one's neighbor. That (neighborly love) is an unspoken agreement. Our community should be one where we naturally have it. Unfortunately, such a thing tends to be excluded in this profit-seeking society. Ultimately, it's a matter of one's values, I believe" (Yamada, Interview).

He provides a positive view of the current state of the village's economic and demographic decline:

"The future (of the local economy) looks gloomy. Economically, it will go toward further decline. Yet, I think there's no need for economic growth. In a sense, I see an ideal picture in the way that European villages are functioning. We can enjoy slow but stable development. There should be a way that we could deal

with sparse population, if the population is really getting smaller. It's OK that the village is going to be a place where retired urban people spend their old age. There are a bunch of empty plots of farmland. We are coming into an aging society. Some people wish to live in the country. It's not always good to have population increase. Look at Katashina.[97] *It's gaining population due to successful tourism development, but they have heaps of garbage and youth crime is increasing"* (Interview).

Another young organic farmer, who moved from Chiba to Kurabuchi with his family a year ago after quitting his previous job as an engineer, provides his perspective with respect to the ideal functioning of the village.

"Perhaps if the village would be specialized in economic performance there would be another result. But it isn't. I am not saying that it's good or bad. If we preserve the aspects of a good rural village, the village will experience further population decline. What is important is a balance (between development and preservation). Farmland preservation is essential for us to sustain agriculture. To some extent, I wish the young would remain in the village. A rural village cannot be talked about solely in economic terms. In big cities there's nothing but income which is important. In a village, this is not always true. People used to be self-sufficient in villages. I know it's impossible to revive such a way of living, but I think such an aspect should be kept to some degree. We don't need too many economic rationalists. I wish people who share the same value would stay or come to this village."

He continues with an environmentalist perspective,

"People's sense of values is the most important thing, I believe—a value to determine whether one seeks an economic profit or environmental preservation. If the latter value is filtered into the hearts of the villagers, then things will go on towards such a direction. Even though some say it's Utopian; it's ideal to live together with nature. However, from the Edo era (a feudal time in Japan) until the present, we've experienced a significant change in the economy. Once we experienced it, we cannot set back time. My ideal is a somewhat intermediate level. ...It's quick to build economic infrastructure, but that would make Kurabuchi a city, not a rural village. Although I have no clear idea, it would be good if we could maintain those living here by preserving the rural environment—a living not solely dependent on economic interests. In the current functioning of capitalism everything depends on values in the market economy, which I don't like. But I have no alternative answer. Everything is determined by capitalism, but the values included in the capital are limited. Does capital consider the value of natural environment? The

---

97 Another village in Tone County, Gunma, located next to Kawaba.

cost of environmental preservation should be considered. Things having no money value have been cut away, which makes the environment worse. If more people would be aware of that, it would be changed" (Interview).

Kondo, the horticultural therapist, also emphasizes the importance of another set of values, and presents his idealistic view on *mura-okoshi*—as one where we are not trapped by a utilitarian value based on short-term economic interests.

"I think we need a different sense of values. It's OK with no population increase. It's OK with fewer young people. But for the aged people's well-being there will be some need for jobs for young people. ...Their (the village office and people) ideas are utilitarian, say, making an onsen, attracting factories, or something. That's it. How about looking at it from a different angle? It takes time. We need (another idea as) software (for development). Having an event is one idea. Then they can sell their products. They need to think about a clever device to sell. To develop manpower, they will need computers. Agriculture involves multiple functions which doesn't only mean selling products. It should contribute to a comprehensive local development. These trends will lead the village to one like German villages, which I consider an ideal. ...Mura-okoshi is considered only from a simplistic view—a merger or survival (with conventional means of rural development). This is an issue prevailing in entire Japan. Mura-okoshi's spending a lot of money doesn't last. The successful cases are those with a different way of thinking, right?" (Interview).

Although what these residents say is highly abstract and idealistic, what they are describing is a scenario that could be called, an eco-welfare village. From their narratives we see a village where organic farmers and environmentally-conscious, disabled, and aged people—together with those who provide support services, such as health and medical practitioners—live.

How can they reach this point? From the interviews, it is apparent that an alternative sense of values is important—I would say a rejection of modernization, including urbanization and industrialization. There is a vague anticipation that, if organic farming and the welfare sector can be successfully established as conventional farming and commerce die out, it is possible that the eco-welfare-related businesses would become a new economic basis for the village. Is this a possible scenario in a capitalist society and in the age of ever-growing globalization?

The village office seems to be considering this option. An eco-tourism project as a means for lifelong educational activity will be proposed in the comprehensive plan for the coming decade. A village official involved in lifelong education programs, who also devotes himself to voluntary activities for child welfare as a leader of an NGO called VYS (The Voluntary Youth Social Workers), informed me that a project will be proposed in which the village is seen as an eco-museum, and villagers play the role of museum staff to welcome urban visitors. (Noboru Tsukakoshi, Village office/VYS, Interview) He adds that no further "hardware development" (infrastructure) will be proposed in the plan.

Many pessimists and few optimists

During my field interviews with 25 different people, I heard many pessimistic views about the future of Kurabuchi, with regard to its economic, social, demographic, and political situations. All interviewees were concerned that economic activity in their village is decreasing, even though most wish to preserve the village's beautiful scenery and environment. Elders of the village say it is sad to see Kurabuchi becoming a village of the elderly. Their favorite village shops are disappearing, and old communal ties and customs are becoming lost. Young Kurabuchi villagers say that the village is not an attractive place to live. For example, a young woman returning to the village from Tokyo confesses:

"The atmosphere of the community is gloomy. I feel no anticipation that something new will begin. It's really backwards in terms of everything. Education is available only up to junior high school here. There are no attractive companies to work at. ...This village isn't moving in a progressive direction. Mergers of villages and townships are in progress, you know. (Economically) this village is already a part of Takasaki (city). Our living basis has been integrated into Takasaki. ...I see no hope in this village. There is no necessity that this village will keep its independence. Rather, it should be merged (into Takasaki). ...When I studied at a school in the countryside of the Netherlands for a year, I was really fascinated by how people nicely take care of traditions from the Middle Ages. In Europe, the old and new are living together well in the actual practice of local development. Yet, here in Japan, it is not the same. I can take no pride in this village. It's shameful" (Noriko Omori, Local bank employee, Interview).

Although many Kurabuchi-born villagers see little hope in the future of their village, it is often newcomers who speak optimistically about the village. The group of newcomers includes organic farmers and horticultural therapists (as described above) as well as a young American from Philadelphia:

"In Japan most places are cities. Few villages remain. Living in a village is valuable. I wish more younger people would stay here. ...What makes Kurabuchi attractive is that it is not urban. That's why people come to Kurabuchi. The village has to resist the desire to make Kurabuchi convenient as a tourist attraction, which would destroy

144

the village environment. They should keep the village the same. Kurabuchi should always be a farming village. Organic farmers make money, and new migrants are coming from cities. I see Kurabuchi as not a suburb. It's still rural. ...It's a perfect distance from cities. Here, there is no crime, no pollution, no traffic jams, but it is not isolated from cities. Preserving village life, history, and the environment is the best way. That makes Kurabuchi attractive. If it were urbanized, we'd lose to the urban. They, I mean cities, are experts in urban stuff. If we (the village) keep our own rules, we can fight against the cities. Imagine if everyone left villages and rushed to cities, they would be overpopulated. I think Kurabuchi won't be a ghost town. Young villagers will come back when they retire. I'm an optimist. 'Inaka' (a Japanese term meaning a countryside) in the United States is very very far from cities. It has to sustain itself. It must help itself. In Japan, villages are like satellites around cities. They're so close (so that they can help each other)" (Michael Wert, English teacher, Living in Kurabuchi for two years, Interview).

As Mr. Wert points out, it is true that Japanese villages, especially in the case of Gunma villages, are not very remote compared to American villages, like those in the Great Plains. In that sense Kurabuchi's future may not be totally hopeless. However, it is a fact that people see and feel their village being left behind in the changing geographical environment, and most see this as not a desirable direction for the majority of the villagers.

10.3. Concluding remarks

Kurabuchi is a village just letting things take their own course. The most probable future, if the village and people do not make any efforts for development, would be further depopulation and economic decline. Surrounded by hills and mountains, Kurabuchi's unfavorable topography hinders the advance of direct urbanization of the village. As village officials point out, regardless of the proximity to big cities, poor transportation still hinders a smooth commute to daily jobs, schools, and medical services in the cities. Depopulation and aging, which are regarded as big issues by most people, continue. The local government, in a sense, accepts this situation, as demonstrated by the absence of strong planning and policy initiatives to counteract it. It seems that they want to maintain the *status quo*.

In this peaceful, quiet place, there is a growing gap between villagers who are adapting successfully and the rest, as economic and social circumstances surrounding Kurabuchi change. While conventional sectors—such as family-operated, subcontracting factories, traditional retail shops, and many Kurabuchi-born farmers—are severely affected by the globalization of production and trade, a small number of people, most of whom are newcomers, are moving in positive directions.

145

As I see it, in the absence of any alternative planning intervention, there might be two other scenarios for the future. First, Kurabuchi could become a suburb of Takasaki city if there were major improvements, including new tunnels and roads, in the basic transportation infrastructure. In this scenario, Kurabuchi would no longer be an old rural village; rather, it would, in a visible way, be swallowed up under the direct influence of capitalism. Second, it could become an eco-welfare village: a village with beautifully preserved nature and with few people. In this scenario, environmentally-sensitive people, including organic farmers (and possibly, for example, artists), retired business workers, patients and disabled people, and health professionals might comprise a major part of the population.

In any case, traditional economic sectors will experience further massive decline and may die out totally. Furthermore, Kurabuchi will not be able to maintain its independence, either economically or administratively. On the one hand, if it were to prosper and enjoy increasing population as a suburban town, it would succeed in maintaining its status as an independent municipality; however, it would be perfectly integrated economically into Takasaki and other neighboring cities. On the other hand, if it were to become a successful eco-welfare village with a small population, under current national policy it would be merged into other neighboring cities. As such, it would only be a part of an (after-merger) greater municipality, and in that case it would be seen by policy makers as a sparsely populated, economically backward region.

The eco-welfare village scenario is not unrealistic. But its anticipated consequences would be further economic and social decline. It would not promise to make people well off, especially those in traditional businesses in the village. Those who speak of this possible direction for the village imply a redefinition of the term, *development*. Conventionally, *development* implies growth and expansion of both the economy and the population. But those who support the eco-welfare scenario question "getting bigger," or "getting richer," as the only goals for development. They all view restoration of autonomous communal ties and neighborly love, as well as environmental preservation, as the most important development objectives. While what they describe may be beautiful, it would mean isolation from the outside.

I must, therefore, pose some questions. Can a community sustain itself, and can people be well-off by rejecting communication with higher-order cultures of production and accumulation? Can villagers achieve a consensus around an anti-modernization development scenario? What the villagers, including old, new, young, aged, and policy planners, really lack in Kurabuchi is communication with each other about the appropriate directions for their community in the future.

146

CHAPTER 11
FROM MULBERRY FIELDS AND CATTLE BARNS TO A BEDROOM COMMUNITY WITH SHOPPING MALLS AND FAST FOOD RESTAURANTS

11.1. Introduction

The last case, that of Ogo township (the Town of Ogo), Seta County, is one of a locality that is moving in a direction completely different from that of any taken by the other five villages located in Gunma's hilly and mountainous regions. Unlike the other villages, Ogo is serving as a frontier for the advance in rural Japan of American-style urban or suburban life. Ogo is undergoing a transformation from an old rural town to a modern suburban town with housing developments, shopping malls, and fast food restaurants. Today—as a result of recent, untamed commercial development in Ogo—there are three major shopping malls and several fast food restaurants, including two MacDonald's. This is a typical form of modern capitalist development found in many places—both in Japan and elsewhere in the world.

Ogo is a municipality with an area of 20km² in the shape of a narrow triangle with a base of 4km and a height of 10km. It includes seven formerly independent villages plus the original Ogo township. These were consolidated in 1889 with the implementation of the modern municipal system by the Meiji imperial government.

Topographically, Ogo is located on the southern foot—a gentle slope—of Mt. Akagi (altitude: 1828m). Unlike the previous five villages, its topography is predominantly flat, and it contains no hilly and mountainous areas, as defined by the Japanese Agricultural Census. Major land uses are farmland (54%), housing (18%), forest (6%), and other uses—including commercial and industrial use—(22%). In general, the southern part of Ogo, where land is mainly designated as an urbanization promotion zone[98] for commercial and housing uses, differs greatly from the northern part, where land use is still largely agricultural. Although this is still generally true, recent unplanned land development has resulted in a more confused pattern of land use.

Historically, Ogo township originated as a local landlord's (the Ogo family's) castle town. It was a prosperous town during early feudal times (A.D. 1400-1500). Although the castle no longer exists, the town prospered as a commercial center of Seta County. Its downtown area—along the original main streets—developed as a commercial district with small retail shops.

Ogo is a place where all roads meet. It can be reached in one hour or less from most major urban areas of Gunma. There is excellent transportation access to Ogo from the prefectural metropolitan area[99] and other major urban areas of Gunma. For example, it is only 10km from Mebashi, the capital city, and 17km from Kiryu (population: 120 thousand). A commuter train connects these cities with Ogo. This convenient location, combined with recent road improvements, has spurred a great demand for housing in Ogo—especially since the 1980s. As an inevitable result of new housing developments, the landscape of the old rural town, which had long prospered as one of the centers of Gunma's sericultural industry, has been transformed.

The current distribution of employment by industrial sector (1995) is as follows: service and the public sector (56%), manufacturing (32%), and agriculture (12%).[100] Per capita income in Ogo is the highest among the six localities in this study. Today, 15,000 people reside in Ogo (1995). The population trend is indicative of the change this locality has been experiencing. Ogo's population grew between 1920 (the year of the first national census) and 1955, but, after World War II and until 1965, it experienced population loss due to outmigration to the cities, just as did other rural villages in Gunma. Since 1970, however, Ogo has consistently experienced a relatively high growth rate.[101] Over that period its population increased by 58%.

---

98 Under the revised Urban Planning Act of 1968.

99 Including the cities of Maebashi (population 285,000) and Takasaki (population 238,000). Maebashi's population is gradually shrinking due to recent migration to its suburbs including Ogo, while Takasaki is still growing at a quite moderate rate.

100 The figure includes those who commute to work outside Ogo.

101 Approximately, 6-12% every fifth census year.

11.2 Description from both a policy and people's perspectives

While many people welcome and enjoy the convenience of modern urban life, some are worried about the loss of traditional communal bonds, moral decay, and a poorer living environment. In this section, I attempt, using the words of several local people and planners from among the 28 interviewees I met, to provide a sketch of the issues raised by this transition.

The main street shopping district

The advance of urbanization with large-scale stores[102] brought to the outskirts of Ogo by outside capital has changed dramatically the landscape of this old rural town—particularly its main street retail community. Ogo's township office lists revitalization of the downtown shopping district, which is becoming less active year by year, as a top-priority issue.

"There is no means for altering the fall of the downtown shopping district due to the advance of large shops along the newly opened bypass roads. The vitalization of the downtown district is our top priority policy" (Akuzawa, Urban Planning Section, Town office, Interview).

Ogo's downtown, with about 50 small retail shops,[103] developed in the area around the Ogo train station along the original main road connecting Maebashi and Isesaki cities. During the feudal era, especially during the 18th Century, Ogo's downtown prospered as the center of the region (current Seta County). Today, more than half of the retail shops on the main street are closed. Commercial activity is shifting from the downtown commercial district to shopping malls, discount shops, and fast-food restaurants along newly opened roads.

An owner of a delicatessen in the downtown area deplores the fact that Ogo consumers have abandoned the old retail community. He once operated a grocery store which he was forced to close due to the advent of large supermarkets. But his current business is not doing very well either. He recalls,

---

102 The direct cause that triggered the advancement of large scale retailers (shopping malls, discount stores, and so on) in Japan was political pressure from the United States. The Japanese government (MITI) had been protecting small retailers through legal measures under the Act for Controlling Large Scale Retail Stores of 1974 (unofficial translation). Based on an agreement reached in official negotiations between the United States and Japan, amendments were passed in 1990 and 1996 that had the effect of liberalizing the legal restrictions on large scale retailers. In 1998, a bill that abolished the act after 2000 was passed.

103 54 shops in 1993 (Arisue 1993: 877). This number should be smaller today.

"Shops have been declining in the last ten years. At first, shops in Maebashi took customers away from us (due to easier transportation that resulted from road improvement). Then big malls came to Ogo. Now our retail shop community is one-sixth of what it was in its heyday, which was about twentyseven or -eight years ago" (Teruaki Maejima, Interview).

He warns that revitalization of the downtown community is critical not only for businesses there, but for a safe community as well,

"What I'm mostly worried about are certain kinds of businesses, such as nightclub businesses,[104] coming here if neglect of the downtown area continues. I'm quite sure that if, say, once just two or three such businesses have settled in, they're going to be a hit. Then the Mafia (yakuza) will come to our town for sure. That's my anxiety. No bank except yakuza finances such businesses. ...Now it's recession. But when the economy begins recovering, they will certainly come to town. That's the easiest business (to happen). The underground people might have investigated which places are mortgaged already" (Maejima, Interview).

Maejima wishes to preserve his community as a healthy place where all families, children, women, and the elderly can walk the streets and enjoy shopping. He has formed a group with five other members that supports retail community revitalization. They have been working on this issue for two years. Regardless of this effort and commitment, Maejima, as well as others, anticipates traditional small shops will all disappear in the near future, which is what he considers to be the worst-case scenario.

Agriculture today

"There are no measures for promoting agriculture. In recent years, some began putting an effort into agritourism, but it doesn't work well. Officially, agricultural promotion is listed as a top policy priority in our third comprehensive plan. However, frankly speaking, it's only an expedient not to discourage the remaining farmers. There's no major farm product in Ogo. It's difficult. You know, Ogo used to prosper as a town of sericulture, which is almost gone now. Today the main functions of Ogo are housing and commerce, actually" (Akuzawa, Town office, Interview).

Ogo was—until the mid 1980s—the last major home of the sericultural industry in Gunma; the Ogo Sericultural Association was finally dissolved two or three years ago. Mulberry fields have been converted to the production of other crops, such as vegetables and field crops, or simply abandoned.

---

104 These are sponsored by yakuza (Japanese Mafia) organizations in many cases in Japan.

Farm land still accounts for more than half of Ogo's land use. About 70% of the gross value of farm output is from livestock and dairy farming, followed by vegetables (about 20%). Today, however, most of the remaining farmers are in their sixties or older, and recent developments of commercial and housing districts along the bypass roads running through the southern part of Ogo have accelerated further the outflow of resources from agriculture. Both young and old farmers whom I interviewed express a pessimistic view of agriculture:

"I have to stay with farming for a while until my daughter grows, because it's the only thing that I can do. ...But, Ogo's livestock production will decline more. It's becoming a bedroom community of Maebashi. Population is steadily growing. It will reach 20 thousand soon. Agriculture is hopeless. It's no good. It's going to be all residential areas" (Tadaichiro Yamaguchi, Hog raiser, Interview).

"For a long time there were 70 families in this Yokozawa district. Now there are 300, as the rural village becomes a bedroom town. Farmers will be disappearing. I used to have livestock, but quit due to housing development surrounding me. Nowadays, agriculture is maintained mostly by the elderly. Such people produce vegetables. So it's difficult to promote agriculture here. I will work on a farm as long as my health permits. But no one's going to take care of the farm after I retire. Most farmers are in their sixties. How many years can they work?" (Masao Fujii, Farmer, 74 years old, Interview).

A manager of the Ogo Agricultural Cooperative admits that the cooperative has given up agricultural promotion. He provides this view :

"Agriculture is disappearing. It will be replaced with housing areas. See, even relatively young farmers are in their sixties! Imagine what will happen ten years from now. ...It means Ogo is blessed with more economic opportunity than, for example, Kurabuchi (where agriculture is still present). It would be ideal if our cooperative could do something like what the Sawada Cooperative does, but we have no experts" (Kaname Yokozawa, Ogo Agricultural Cooperative, Interview).

Local railroads

Of the six localities investigated in this study, only Ogo is served by a train. The Jomo Electric Railway Company (*Jomo Dentetsu*) runs between the cities of Maebashi and Kiryu, connecting townships and villages in Seta County and providing passenger service by commuter train. Ogo station was opened in 1927. The railway—like other local train services running in non-metropolitan areas of Japan—has been severely affected by the advance of motorization. Consequently it has lost its role as a major part of the public transportation system. The train today is an old-fashioned means of transportation. Passengers are likely to be high school age children commuting to schools in other districts in the region and the elderly who cannot drive by themselves.

A former employee of the railway company recalls,

"As the automobile has become commonplace, the train company has come to difficulty. There used to be 300 employees. Now it's downsizing to 120. We can do nothing during these times. It's natural. You know, we used to live in a time when we had no TVs and air conditioners, but we all have those today. ...The best times for the train company were up until 20 years ago. I remember how at that time trains were so busy and packed with passengers. A national subsidy for local train services was abolished two years ago. Now municipalities (where the Jomo train runs) provide financial assistance according to the number of passengers per municipality. And the company is rationalizing management by selling real estate and reducing employee numbers. Although people complain about train fares, which are high, I still retain an intimate feeling with the train" (Matsugoro Ito, Travel Agent/Formerly train company employee, Interview).

The price of rapid urbanization: Confusion over land use and a lack of basic infrastructure

"This town is growing too fast, too soon. It quickly changed from a small rural village to a city. So the village office couldn't keep up with the change. They should have considered it. I think they could have. They did it in a haphazard manner" (Eiko Sudo (Ms.), Housewife, Interview).

Today, Ogo's growth is based on housing and large-scale commercial developments. Ogo's location is convenient for commuting to any city in Gunma. Relatively cheap land prices in Ogo bolster demand for housing developments there. Road improvements attract newcomers who seek affordable housing and who work in other Gunma Prefecture cities. After 1975, the village's population rapidly increased at a rate of 6-12% every five years due largely to its function as a bedroom community for Maebashi. During the 1988-1997 period, 108ha of farmland were converted—mainly to housing and commercial use. This means that there was a 10% loss of farmland in the past decade.

During my field interviews people identified several problems that are a consequence of rapid growth in population and changes in the social and economic functions of Ogo. They see three main problem areas: 1) confused patterns of land use, 2) poor branch roads in residential districts, and 3) neglected investment in educational facilities.

In the first place, there has been no systematic attempt to regulate land use, and this has resulted in chaotic land use patterns. A walk around Ogo reveals, for example, a cattle barn surrounded by residential houses built close together, or a small housing development in paddy fields. A hog-raising farmer complains,

"This community has a new incoming family every month or every week. There are 90 families here now, while there were only 60 five years ago. Since pigs smell bad, we have a new environmental situation between the farmers and newcomers. ...We didn't have such a problem until 10 years ago. But our neighborhood has grown nearly up to 100 families as a new road is being built. I've thought that my business is still OK, but the reality is hard on us. Individual effort (for reducing pollution from livestock) is essential. But why are houses allowed to be built in the manner of one after another in an area designated for agricultural promotion like this one? Zoning doesn't work neatly" (Tadaichiro Yamaguchi, Interview).

Another consequence of rapid and untamed urban development is insufficient basic living infrastructure. Thus, in the second place, both original residents and newcomers point to poorly provided branch roads and a shortage of children's playgrounds.

"An assemblyman elected from this hamlet, who runs a construction company, says this district's going to be all housing soon. But, you see, (branch) roads (in residential hamlets) are so poor. They do not satisfy an official construction standard in terms of width. No playground is provided while the young population increases. A road in front of my house had long been unpaved and had no drainage function, so it became a river when rain fell. It's really crude housing development" (Hiromi Matsui (Ms.), Housewife/dietitian, Interview).

"While there's heavier traffic and more perverts in town, there are no playgrounds or places where children can play safely. Very few such facilities are provided. I know many newcomers complain about it. Newly developed houses look poor. No (branch) roads, where a vehicle can be driven safely, have been made" (Eiichi Ohara, Real estate management, Interview).

In all, it is observed that both farmers and non-farmers are suffering badly from inadequate town planning during this period of rapid change in land use and the transformation of the social and economic functions of the town.

In the third place, there is concern about spending on education. Throughout the field interviewing in Ogo, this was the most frequent complaint about the village office: poor spending for education.[105] Improvement of

---

105 In Japan, compulsory education consists of elementary school (six years) and junior high school(3 years); these public school facilities are financed and managed by a municipal government (village, town, or city office); whereas teachers at public schools are employed and appointed by a prefectural government.

school facilities is an urgent issue. For example, there are three elementary schools in Ogo: The Ogo School (883 students), Takikura School (240), and Takikura Branch School (20). The Ogo School serves the southern part of Ogo, in which urbanization has greatly taken over.

"I was really surprised at the poor school facility in Ogo when I came. No building improvements have been made in the last thirty years, while the number of students has grown three times. The tap water is brown! Male and female students still share the same bathroom! There're a lot of leaks in the roof" (Mariko Ohara, Interview).

"The school facility is too old and too small. ...The Ogo Elementary School has had no improvements made to it in 30 years. ...I feel sorry for children at the Ogo school with such poor facilities compared with the other one. It's not fair that there's such a huge gap in the educational environment in the same municipality. For example, the same number of computers, say, two or four, are provided to each school, regardless of such a huge difference in student numbers. When I visited a school in Niisato village[106] for a P.T.A. meeting, I saw that they have a computing lab and an English-learning lab. We have neither in Ogo. We have no money for education, because it goes to trunk ("interstate") roads and public buildings. They (one of the Niisdato participants) sneeringly said 'I'm sorry. Ogo doesn't spend money on education.' Educational investment is essential to foster children" (Eiko Sudo, Interview).

Juvenile delinquency

Akuzawa, a town official, calls attention to an increase in juvenile delinquency and crime as another negative consequence of rapid urbanization and the influx of new migrants from cities. There are Ogo-based delinquent groups. Several interviewees, both parents and high school students, mentioned this. Teachers at the Ogo Junior High School admit that police are dispatched to commencement ceremonies due to student riots against teachers which occurred in the past. Kikuchi, a teacher at the Ogo Junior High School, observes that youth delinquency in Ogo was already above average compared with other rural municipalities in the same county when he taught in Ogo ten years ago, so that this is not a very recent phenomenon. Statistics from the Ogo Police Station support his observation; reported juvenile delinquency has been consistently in the range of 200-400 cases per year, with an average of 329 cases per year during the past ten years (1989-1998).[107]

---

106 Another village in Seta County.

107 I am not prepared to judge how serious the problem of juvenile delinquency is in Ogo compared with other cities in Japan. It can easily be assumed, however, that

What's Ogo's identity?

"What *is* Ogo's identity?" "What assets does Ogo have?" For people in Ogo, these simple questions are not easy to answer. In the other five villages, regardless of the actual socio-economic situations people faced, their most common answer was simply its "rural environment" or "nature." In Ogo, the most frequent answers to this question are "none" or "I don't know." Two people spoke about their nostalgic feeling for the pride of an old castle town. In this regard, a local businessman running an Ogo-based apparel company suggests the following:

"I was born and grew up in Ogo, but I have dealers all over the county. What really saddens me, as a resident of Ogo, is that no one knows about this town. It's less than 1%. Most people know Maebashi or Takasaki, but no one knows this place. Let me tell you a story which happened to me some time ago. I was asked by one of our dealers, whom I had known for a long time, in Kanagawa Prefecture: 'By the way, where is your company located?' I was very sad to hear this. Even Ueno village has more fame than Ogo. My town is one in which we can take pride. It's not a matter of whether it is big or small, rich or poor. Can you tell that a man who earns fifty million yen[108] a year is happier than a man who only earns five million?[109] I can't. In Ogo a policy is discussed without a philosophy, without thoughtfulness. So, no one can answer the question: What's Ogo's identity?" (Masao Fujii, Interview).

A call for a human dimension to development: Insightful comments from community leaders

Rapid change has brought some negative phenomena, such as youth crime, pollution from livestock due to poor land use regulation, garbage problems, loss of close communal ties, and so forth—most of which are common urban problems found elsewhere in Japan. They seem to be a common tradeoff for a modern, convenient life. A number of insightful comments on these matters were made by interviewees—some of whom play a leadership role in the community.

---

the problem of juvenile crime in Ogo, as in Japan generally, is far less serious than it is in the United States. The reason for paying attention to it here is that, of the six municipalities I studied, only in Ogo was juvenile delinquency spoken of as a serious issue by both planners and citizens. Consequently I view this as a defining characteristic of Ogo relative to the other localities.

108 Approximately, US$420,000.
109 Approximately, US$42,000.

Firstly, the local businessman, Fujii, feels that local political leaders—in fact the citizenry as a whole—lack something important, which may be pride in their home town, or a vision for its future.

"Probably in the past and future, no novel idea has come or will come up in this town, I think. ...They (the town office and local politicians) lack a comprehensive vision. They just waste tax money. I see no vision in their spending for new roads. A company must have a philosophy in their business; but the government (town office) doesn't. They have no mission statement, which, I believe, is the most important thing. They need to draw up a future plan to show others. Of course, there will always be an objection by some to doing something new, but to answer these objections it is necessary (for the town office) to have a mission statement. They do everything with tactics, but with no strategy. In its current direction, Ogo will function just as a bedroom community (as a suburb of Maebashi). But, have we considered what sort of town we desire? That's the essential element. Since we lack that, this town is just drifting on and on without having a clear direction. For example, how do we deal with the water supply shortage; with schools crowded with children (due to population growth)? It's a difficult thing to solve, unless we develop our ideal, which should be the starting point" (Fujii, Interview).

An implication of these remarks is that it is the human dimension which should lead development efforts and direct Ogo in a more desirable direction. Nobuyuki Inoue, a young dairy farmer (age: 41), seconds this opinion. As a board member of the local P.T.A. Inoue emphasizes the importance of education as a goal of development—in the true sense of the term,

"It's impossible for an individual a community to alter the direction the Japanese economy is heading, you know. Big business will prosper. That's the way of this capitalist society. It cannot be helped. Then, what happens when we totally depend on that? They only sell the goods everyone demands. However, there should be community-based business. In the current way, small business is losing. Of course, it's very good to have a convenient life. So, realistically, it's important to respond to diverse consumer needs. That's what I want to say. I mean, essentially we live together by helping each other, but in reality everyone forgets it. For example, we need a quiet environment in some place, in other words, a quiet village or a quiet residential district. You know, it only takes 15 minuets to be in (the fringe of) Maebashi from Ogo. That's OK. Big shops are coming and competing among themselves. It's not for the community. This is half the reason that big stores come here. Therefore, they may leave suddenly if it doesn't pay. For us, this community is a quiet rural town, a place where people can enjoy hobby farming on Sundays, for example. Our community would be better if we can have more close communication among ourselves. ...Our children should be

brought up, taken care of by the community, in a voluntary manner. I don't think it's a healthy community where children shut themselves in a house for computer games and old people get together for gateball,[110] *where there's no communication between the young and old. I want to get back the intimate communications we used to have before. We lack even a minimum level of communication. My ideal is a society without too much consumption. We need to ask ourselves: For what do I work? I want my job to be part of my life's dream. In this sense, the current direction of Japanese society is too confining. So, what is most important for Ogo's development is educating people. It's people who create everything"* (Nobuyuki Inoue, Dairy farmer, Interview).

Another community leader shares the same opinion. Hisashi Ebara taught fine arts for 40 years at junior high schools in the County. Now, after retirement, he is organizing various community groups for cultural and educational activities, while he also engages in farming. He speaks of a dichotomous situation where there are two opposite developments occurring: material development and moral decline—both the consequence of modernization and urbanization.

"Without a doubt, Ogo is moving in the direction of urbanization. It brings with it "development" in a material, economic sense, while I see a retrogression in people's morality. Hence, the education of people is important. Now, I am undertaking the role of chair of the Cultural Association of Ogo (Ogo Bunka Kyokai). There is some growing awareness of lifelong education and preserving our festivals. A theatrical group formed two years ago with 36 members, including children and the elderly. That's part of education. ...I don't think we need new roads. That's not the most important thing. You may say I'm too conservative, old-fashioned, but I want to value good old traditions. In Japan, I think we haven't understood the real meaning of democracy, liberalism, or egalitarianism. Real democracy should begin with an individual as a member of a community taking responsibility. In this sense, what we believed democracy was after the war is wrong.[111] *...It's only egoism"* (Ebara, Interview).

Regardless of his current commitment, Ebara has a pessimistic view of the future of Ogo with respect to his vision of development.

---

110 A cricket-like ball game which is a popular leisure sport with the elderly in Japan. You will see it played on many playgrounds in Japan.

111 It is appropriate to supplement his comment here. While Mr. Ebara values and respects democracy in the true sense of the word, he believes that the democracy imported from the United States after World War II has not functioned appropriately in Japan because of the absence of the concept of political citizenship and the prevalence of a mentality oriented to economics.

"It's going to be even more of a bedroom town and part of Maebashi—one of the residential regions on the periphery of the (Tokyo) metropolitan area. I'm pessimistic in terms of the morality of the people. The only thing I can do at my best is to make a small effort for cultivating colleagues who share the same idea."

"History judges everything"

As Fujii, the farmer, mentions, it is true that no one can change the current direction of capitalist development, which is transforming the social and economic functions, spatial structures, culture, and lifestyles in this (ex-) rural town. To close this section, it is appropriate to quote an interviewee who believes, insightfully, that history judges everything:

"What we really need is our own culture. That's where we can begin something. What is wrong is that we ourselves don't make any self-effort. So, it's helpless if the current Ogo is lost in the (contemporary) times. Once it happens, then we should learn something from it—from which Ogo can be reborn" (Kosuke Takai, Insurance agent, Interview).

11.3 Concluding remarks

I see Ogo as a place, such as those found elsewhere on the periphery of metropolitan areas in Japan, that is tossed about by the powerful influence of modern capitalist development. The story of Ogo is not unique; similar stories may be found elsewhere on the frontier as this sort of development takes place. The outcome was not planned. Nevertheless there may be a hidden political motive of local policy makers and planners: namely, to attract that change in order to force economic development. This was not mentioned enough during the field interviews. For instance, this consequence—a further extension of the core into the periphery—should have been anticipated when new roads were planned.

Regardless of what citizens of Ogo may want, the next decade will certainly see the completion of Ogo's transition from a rural town to a typical suburban city—a residential and commercial district that is simply an extension of the urban core. And this would be its primary social and economic function. There will be few remaining farmers; abandoned farmland will be converted into residential areas, with some, perhaps, preserved as community allotment gardens (which does not work well, in a true sense of the term, in Kurabuchi). In any case, the downtown community will experience further decline, while the locality continues to grow in a more conventional way. This may be an inevitable consequence of one contemporary form of capitalist development.

The experience of Ogo suggests some valuable implications when considering the earlier cases. Some may pose the question: If, with a vigorous political will, people had attempted to preserve Ogo's rural identity, would it have worked, as it did, for example, in Kawaba? My answer is no. Ogo is much more directly and strongly influenced by nearby metropolitan regions than is Kawaba by the city of Numata. It lacks good tourism resources. It also lacks valuable planning expertise found in the previous three. There is no political will to preserve rural identity as a means of sustaining the community in Ogo. Hence, various external and internal factors made this locality naturally choose a *laissez faire* policy with respect to local development. This assures "growth" through an intensification of the commercial and residential functions of the locality. This process assures capital accumulation for outside capitalists, including supermarket companies, restaurant chains, and private housing developers. In the meantime, local businesses, including the retail community, farmers, and even the local railway company are consistently the losers.

One high school student describes this phenomenon as "modernization" (Masako Okada, Interview), and another high school student says "urbanization means development" (Yuki Inoue, Interview). But an older farmer/retired teacher sees it as "material development with moral decadence" (Ebara, Interview).

From one perspective, the situation of Ogo is the flip side of the coin, if we compare it with Ueno. The two stories suggest the following conclusion: It is not an easy task for a locality to find a way to swim against the powerful wave of spatial differentiation as one result of contemporary capitalist development.

CHAPTER 12
SUMMARY AND REFLECTIONS

"The irony is that tradition is now often preserved by being commodified and marketed. ...historical tradition is recognized as a museum culture...of local history, of local production, ...and integrated into a long-lost and often romanticized daily life" (Harvey 1990: 303).

General observations

In this book, I have relied on extensive field work, during which I interviewed both citizens—from various walks of life and varying political persuasions—and public officials and planners. I have used these citizen and official observations and explanations, together with my own interpretations, to describe the changes that are occurring in six Gunma villages in response to global economic forces. I have also used them to record the policy responses of village officials and the reactions of local citizens both to the changes themselves and to village policy.

I have demonstrated a number of place/space contradictions. The stories of these six rural localities demonstrate that rural communities on the periphery of Tokyo—a global city, with the world's largest urban agglomeration—are experiencing social, economic, and ultimately spatial differentiation in which they are differentiated from each other—i.e. that they have each responded *differently* to the contemporary capitalist dynamic.

In addition, as my own observation, I would like to point to an aspect of the geography that is often ignored: a rural area as "relative space" with respect to urban (and fundamentally global) economic influences. My point here is that there are no absolute rural villages in terms of the *space* of capital accumulation. Rather, villages are all—in an economic sense—relative

160

entities in the geography of an urban-rural continuum (see Chapter 1), regardless of existing physical/topographical and/or political/administrative boundaries. This is in accord with the teaching of New Urban Economics. This is reflected in the fact that many interviewees' interests (aside from those of a few environmentalists) are expressed in terms of attracting urban money or connecting their businesses and lives with cities (commuting, shopping, and so on).[112]

Comparing the six localities

Is it possible for rural localities to retain their rural identities? Or will they just drift—simply accommodating to the changing geography? How, if it is at all possible, can a locality plan to achieve economic development while preserving its rural identity, and thus to resist the forces of economic decline and/or dissolution into the urban agglomeration? What factors account for the success or failure of some localities in achieving economic development while retaining their rural identities? And what distinguishes those communities that are (or promise to be) successful from those that aren't?

Table 1 summarizes comparative advantages and disadvantages in economic, political, geographical endowments, and so forth of the six cases. As we have seen, the first three localities, Sawada, Kawaba, and Niiharu, have been successful—at least with respect to preserving their rural identities. They have created new sources of employment for their villagers; and, to some extent, they have been successful in stabilizing their populations. Although these three cases exhibit variations in development (and preservation) patterns due to differences in locational advantages and other natural endowments, nevertheless, they also display an important common element: they all adopted development models in which they would directly benefit from the resources of urban areas, including the people themselves, their knowledge, and capital. None of the three would have been able to develop, or at least to revitalize its economy, while simultaneously preserving its rural identity without this positive urban influence.

Despite the fact that I was able to identify three cases of villages that have been successful in achieving economic development, population stabilization, the preservation of their rural identities, a major conclusion of my research is, that *the factors that made these three villages successful were, in a sense exceptional.* I conclude, therefore, that *their model cannot be generalized to every rural village.*

---

112 In this sense, rural villages are not the same—with respect to social functions, production roles, and social classes—as those that Marx saw in the nineteenth century. The classical urban-rural dichotomy is useful typology only when we speak of a particular historical period of capitalist development—one which, in modern industrial societies, no longer exists.

These exceptional factors include the following:

- Multiple and broad local economic and business opportunities (including tourism resources) that can attract residents, knowledge, and capital from surrounding urban areas.

- Good transportation. This makes urban job markets accessible to villagers, and it makes the villages accessible to urban residents for recreational purposes (Kawaba, Niiharu).

- Special local products that can be marketed in specialized urban consumer markets (Sawada, Kawaba).

In addition, the first three villages have certain advantages in human resources:

- Exogenous and endogenous planning expertise and knowledge (Kawaba, Niiharu).

- Political leadership and strong planning authorities.

Because of these exceptional factors, the villages in the first three case studies were able to find ways to adapt effectively to the changing geography. For example, good planning made it possible for Niiharu to strengthen its economic base as well as to preserve its rural identity. It did this through tourism development and the promotion of tourism-friendly agriculture; by attracting an R&D center and production plant of an automobile firm; and by providing public housing for residents commuting to cities.

However, I hold that these models are even more restricted in their usefulness. Not only do they apply only to villages that are endowed with exceptional resources, but even within that set of villages, only a limited number—namely, *those with the "most exceptional resources"—can apply this model successfully over the long-run*. The reason for this is that this model will inevitably—now or in the future—place those villages that use it in competition with each other. Their current success is a result of a market environment in which competition is limited. Limited competition has thus far assured the scarcity of their resources—including historic resources, a country landscape, agricultural commodities, and *onsen*. However, continued scarcity is not guaranteed in the long-run, should other villages adopt the same approach—perhaps improving upon it in some ways. Thus, the villages I studied are in the position of the early bird that catches the worm.[113]

---

113 Schumpeter's theory of the dynamics of competition, specifically, the waves of destructive forces of market competition, is relevant here (See Schumpeter 1983 and 1994).

Table 1: Six Localities Compared

	Sawada	Kawaba	Niiharu	Ueno	Kurabuchi	Ogo
COMPARATIVE (DIS)ADVANTAGES						
Urban proximity /transportation infrastructure	++	+++	+++	+	++	++++
Economic opportunities*	+++	+++	+++	+	++	++++
Tourism resources	+++	+++	++++	++	+	+
Strategic intent /Political will	++++	++++	+++	+++	+	+
Exogenous planning expertise/knowledge	+++	++++	++++	+	++	+
Dominant technologies and industries**	Small farming, Small business, Food processing	Small farming, Small business	R&D, Branch plant, Small business, Small farming	Hand craft, Construction labor, Small business	Organic farming, Branch plant, Small business	Big business, Small farming
CONSEQUENCES of CURRENT TRENDS						
Demographic trend	Moderate decrease	Moderate increase	Moderate decrease	Progressive decrease	Progressive decrease	Progressive increase
Rural environment	-	-	-	-	-	Worsened
Major planning issues	Aging, Depopulation	Temptation of urbanization, Building consensus on the Setagaya-Kawaba exchange programs, Aging	Onsen revitalization, Building consensus for village-park project, Aging	Depopulation, Community extinction, Aging	Depopulation, Aging, Abandoned farmland, Industrial evacuation	Downtown revitalization, Juvenile delinquency, Untamed housing development, confused land use, Poor living environment
FUTURE						
Expected scenario	Current situation continued	Current situation continued	Current situation continued	Progressive decline	Progressive decline	Untamed urban sprawls

*Including those available in neighboring urban areas.

**Tourism and public services excluded.

The number of "+" indicates the degree of a comparative advantage.

Thus, over the long-run, as more villages attempt to apply this model, only a limited number—those with the *most exceptional* resources—can survive. This is a second reason why this strategy is incapable of generalization to all villages.

While three villages have been successful, at least in the short-term, in making economic adaptations that have enabled both a stabilization of their populations and the preservation of their rural identities, the last three localities—Ueno, Kurabuchi, and Ogo—have been unsuccessful. Either they have failed to maintain a stable population or industrial/economic base (two measures of economic development) and/or they have failed to preserve their landscapes and rural environment.

In its struggle for village revitalization, Ueno's attempt resembles the struggles of the first three villages, but its location is likely to make its efforts unsuccessful. Thus, with respect to one of the "exceptional factors" that had a positive effect in the former three cases, namely the degree of urban influence, Ueno's location makes it too remote. Kurabuchi lacks the enabling factors of strong political leadership and planning expertise. It is still struggling to find a desirable direction for the future. Finally, Ogo's proximity to the urban core makes it improbable that it can reverse a trend toward suburbanization and absorption into the urban core. Ironically, while Ueno's location makes it too remote to be successful, Ogo is too close. While Ogo is experiencing economic "development" through its developing peripheral relationship with the urban core, the cost of this development is loss of its rural identity.

A note on defining development

My research reveals that not all citizens view "development" in conventional terms. Some interviewees raised this fundamental question: What is development? Although the views of those who question the conventional definition of "development" seemed to me to be idealistic, I also see some insightful vision in their narratives. Nevertheless, this segment of the population is in the minority. As a result it would not be possible to develop a consensus in their respective communities around their vision of development.

The case of Ogo demonstrates the problematic nature of the conventional definition of "development." Ogo is experiencing successful economic development in the conventional sense. It is attracting new commercial businesses, building new housing, and experiencing growth in population. However, Ogo's development also demonstrates the negative trade-off's implied in the conventional model and the contradictions of modernization:

the abandonment of its identity as a rural village, increased crime, and threats to the environment, including negative land-use impacts.[114]

The majority of the people I interviewed for this study believe that economic development and an expanding population are top priorities. However, at the same time most people have strong feelings about preserving their village's rural identity. The question is *whether it is possible to achieve both*. This important question will be the subject of the of remainder this book.

Concluding comments

To close Part II, my general conclusion from the case studies is that a rural development model based on traditional concepts of "rural," including tourism and amenities—often referred to as *mura-okoshi*—should not be an essential or primary planning strategy for villages that are attempting to address the problem of uneven rural development. Today, many rural municipalities in Japan view tourism promotion as a panacea for local economic and agricultural revitalization. Clearly, it is impossible for all villages to follow that model. Consequently, assuming the twin objectives of sustainable economic development and maintenance of rural identity, planners must look to other strategies for achieving these goals.

My insights into this question, gained from intensive study of six villages in Gunma that are struggling with the forces of change that accompany global capitalism, are as follows:

(1) The changes, driven by global capitalism, are inevitable. Regardless of their own will, wishes, and efforts, people and planners cannot stop this change. Change will occur. Often it will occur in destructive ways;

(2) The question, then, is not whether or not to change, but rather how to channel this change and transform rural village economies so that

    (a) residents achieve a growing standard of living, taking into account both economic and non-economic values;

    (b) the village population base either grows or is, at least, stabilized;

---

114 Of course, the meaning of the term, development, differs according to people's region, country, or community of residence, values, age, sex, and occupation. As may be appreciated from the above, there is no absolute poverty in rural Japan—such as that found widely in the rest of Asia, other third world regions, and even in other industrialized states like the United States. This is true even of a "backwards" community like Ueno. Nor is there illiteracy among the people in Japanese mountain villages, even among those with only a secondary education. In addition, downtown Ogo is still safe enough for ordinary citizens and children to live. In this sense, these villages are all "developed."

(c) The benefits and costs of these changes are distributed "fairly;" and

(d) The rural environment (or identity) is preserved.

I conclude from my case studies that, although some villages have been successful in applying "*mura-okoshi*" models to achieve these goals, this approach will be successful only in "exceptional" cases in the short-run; in the long-run, these models are even more limited in applicability. That means that we must look elsewhere for effective development models for rural villages in the age of the global economy in which, left unchecked, forces will either destroy both the economic basis of rural villages and, therefore, the villages themselves as "places;" or villages will survive economically, but they will lose their identities as rural places as they are absorbed into their urban cores. The remainder of this book focuses on one such possible alternative.

PART THREE

CONCLUSIONS

CHAPTER 13
A NEED FOR AN ALTERNATIVE
PLANNING PERSPECTIVE

Good planning for a better society

I would like to lay out some fundamental propositions about the role and purposes of planning.

I propose the following definitions of "good planning." (1) Good planning aims at slowing down catastrophic change, and assisting in adaptation to it. Thus, the purpose of planning is not to stop history, but rather to assist in adapting to it. (2) Good planning aims to move ahead of change and to gain control over its direction, not to stop it. (3) Good planning aims to promote social choices such that the best human qualities—those which had given meaning to community life in the past—can be carried over into the future, and, through adaptation, survive in the new, historically changed environment.

Again, what is mura-okoshi?

I must add another definition to the Japanese term, *mura-okoshi*, which refers to a type of local self-development movement in Japanese villages and towns: *mura-okoshi* is a locality's (contradictory) struggle against history—in this case modernization in the context of global capitalism. These forces affect the community's economy, society, and physical environment—i.e., its rural identity. Many of the struggles to develop that employ *mura-okoshi* strategies will be "losing battle(s)," as noted by a New Zealander in Ueno, because (as I will argue throughout this and the following chapters) they ignore the

169

strength and importance of historic forces for change. Planners must begin to pay serious attention to these forces in planning for the future of rural villages.

If what has been defined as "successful *mura-okoshi*" is village revitalization through self-commodification" of local resources and environment[115]— which is typically attained by tourism—villages will be forced to compete in the market on the basis of their rural identities. Thus, *mura-okoshi* is a competition among villages unwittingly organized by local authorities. Not only do these strategies promote potentially destructive competition, but in terms of the above characteristics of good planning, *mura-okoshi* fails to address the disadvantages and negative effects on rural villages of their spatial and economic situations.

Mura-okoshi promoters, including local politicians, planners, and those officials at higher levels who provide political and financial support to these efforts through various subsidy and grant programs, are attempting to deal with the contradictions of modernization. Ironically, however, *mura-okoshi* strategies may only reinforce those contradictions. In this sense, the *mura-okoshi* movement in Japan cannot be viewed as a post-modern solution to the problem of uneven regional differentiation.[116]

Among policy makers and planners of rural development in Japan, there is still a widespread tendency to perceive rural communities as separate from cities, and not to see the broader scope of regional development (a place-oriented mind). Thus planners are still trapped by the classical model of the Weberian urban-rural dichotomy, which ignores the more complex and relational space/place interactions and dynamics. And conventional arguments on the problem of rural decline have tended to view the issue principally from a narrow agro-food perspective.

The need for an alternative planning paradigm

My case studies have demonstrated that even successful examples of rural development or *mura-okoshi* strategies, such as strengthening and connecting the agro-food and tourism sectors, will typically not attract a younger, productive population to the villages.[117] In Ueno and Kurabuchi, the problem

---

115 Goto (1993) defines new countryside enterprises (organic farmers, handcraftsmen, countryside inns, folk culture performers, and so forth) for mura-okoshi as "commodification from within" (26).

116 Goto (1993) states that some (both governments and scholars in Japan) find hope for "a positive step toward a post-industrial society" in advocating "endogenous development for a small locality" (21-23).

117 Highly profitable commercial agriculture may be another possible means. Yet it is unrealistic to assume small subsistence farming in mountain villages could be re-born

of a shrinking agricultural sector has been compounded by the loss of branch and subcontracting firms—the kinds of activities that could have provided jobs for youthful workers. Since sustained economic development in rural villages depends upon the village's ability to attract and maintain a stable or growing population of these younger workers, *mura-okoshi* efforts, built primarily on the village's natural endowments, are unlikely to attract or build the workforce for "real" development—i.e., rising standards of living shared more generally by residents throughout each village.

The underlying issue that must be addressed by planners in village revitalization/development policy is the contradiction between space and place. While place-based planning (such as *mura-okoshi*) focuses on maintaining the identity of rural villages from some past period, the present economic dynamic is forcing villages into a space governed ultimately by global economic forces. In other words, while the *mura-okoshi* planning paradigm adheres to a notion of place and place-based practices, the spatial organization of Gunma villages has been changing considerably. Good planning practice cannot ignore this spatial dynamic. If, as we assume, the role of planners is to shape existing forces in such a way as to promote a society in which, among other things, people in every region and in every social class are assured the right to a decent standard of living, planners must both understand the forces that are transforming village spatial identities and incorporate them into their development planning. They cannot ignore them in favor of place-based strategies and expect to promote sustainable development, including rising standards of living that are widely shared among village residents.

All Gunma villages have their own traditions and cultures. Everyone presently living in these villages is, to some extent, influenced by village history and traditions. Villages and towns are physical entities, bounded by mountains and rivers and divided administratively by municipal boundaries. A village is a receptacle for people to live and work (produce); it is a place where past, present, and (possibly) future meet through people's daily social, economic, and political activities. All of these are place-based characteristics and practices. But, a village is also a spatially relative entity; in the broader context of economic location, it is always influenced—and even controlled— by higher-order systems of production and capital accumulation. Gunma's rural localities are directly linked to their urban cores—principally to regional metropolitan centers such as Maebashi and Takasaki and a few other neighboring cities—but ultimately to Tokyo—and beyond that to the "space of flow" of the global economy (Castells 1992). Considerations of space take

---

in such a way, considering the domestic and global food and agriculture regimes.

us far beyond place boundaries and physical distances to global economic forces and activities and to global flows of money, information, and people.

Planning strategies in the case studies do not attempt to control or shape these spatial forces—and thus they cannot deal effectively with spatial unevenness. Each village (with the exception of Ogo) places a high priority on preserving its local culture, environment, amenity, and traditional economic sectors (place variables); planners and local officials consider development based on preservation and enhancement of "place" to be the best—perhaps the only—means for rural revitalization. In so doing, they largely ignore the socio-spatial aspect of the modern capitalist society. Ironically, such planning threatens to lock these villages in a spatial periphery—where they would continue to employ the same old place-bound methods of production.

I have previously critiqued this approach by noting its limited applicability—namely to only those villages with the most exceptional natural conditions—and to only a limited number of people within these localities who participate in the few targeted (usually agritourism) activities. More generally, in terms of good planning practice, such planning limits rural opportunities to old technologies and practices. With this kind of planning, the community can be expected to remain rural and its residents to continue to play a traditional role in the spatial division of labor. It is doubtful that this is in the best interests of the majority of people in the village (as my interviews tend to confirm), and, therefore, it is doubtful that this is consistent with good planning practice. Regardless of place, people have a right to choose how they wish to live. Good planning should attempt to offer them that choice.

APPENDIX A
CATEGORY OF EXPECTED
INTERVIEWEES

(A List shown to local counterparts in Gunma)[118]

Category A: Local Residents
Office/factory workers
-commuting to an office/factory within the village (township)
-commuting to an office/factory outside the village (township)
Migrants from cities
Local students (senior high school or upperclassmen preferred)
Housewives
-moved in from other regions
-locally born
Retail shop owners
School teachers
Young people in their twenties (preferably not in public service)
Farmers
-Relatively young full-time farmers
-Part-time farmers (including retired/aged)

Category B: Planners, officials, and policy makers
Municipal office
Chamber of commerce
Tourist office
Agricultural/forestry cooperative
Assemblymen
Professional consultants/advisors to village (township)

---

118 This list was prepared as a wish list for selecting interviewees. Hence it is not
mandatory, and each sub-category is not necessarily mutually exclusive.

APPENDIX B
INTERVIEW SHEETS

The following questions were prepared as an interview guide. However, actual interviews were sometimes conducted in a relatively flexible manner and the pre-designated questions were not rigidly adhered to.

<u>Questionnaire</u>

(For citizens, but also occasionally used for planners/policy makers)

CURRENT SITUATION
• What do you like/dislike about:
-the way the village (township) is functioning today?
-the direction in which the village (township) is moving?
• Why do you like/dislike it?

DEVELOPMENT PROBLEMS
• What should be done in addition to current development/preservation efforts?
• What should be changed and how?

INDIVIDUAL VALUES
• What are your village's (township's) basic values for living and what are your own personal values for living?
• What are your priorities, in terms of development/preservation of the village?
• As a villager, what currently concerns you the most (what are the problems) about the village (township), regarding all aspects of living there?
• In general, it is reported that there has been a growing awareness of the value of rural areas from the perspectives of environment, ecology, amenity, and so forth. As a rural resident, how do you perceive this?

FUTURE
• What would be the ideal functioning of the village (township) today and in the future (e.g., 10, 20, and 30 years into the future)?
• How can the village (township) get to that point?

Questions for planners, officials, and policy makers

• What are the assets (advantages) of your village?
• What are the disadvantages of your village?
• What was the beginning of your mura-okoshi initiative? How did the village begin it?
• Tell me something about the planning process of your efforts/ programs.
• Is there someone who plays a significant leadership role in the planning of your development/preservation efforts?
• What major information sources did the village use?
• Where do the major financial sources of the programs come from?
• Are there any other key individuals in the community?
• What makes your mura-okoshi a lasting program?
• What do you think about the sustainability of your efforts (programs) and the future of the village?

BIBLIOGRAPHY

Arisue, Takeo. 1993. *Shichoson-betsu Gunma-ken no Chishi* (Gunma's Topography of Cities, Towns, and Villages). Meabashi: Chiiki-kagaku-kenkyusho. (In Japanese)

Barkin, David. 1998. *Wealth, Poverty and Sustainable Development.* Mexico: Centro de Ecología y Desarrollo, A., C.

Bensman, Joseph. 1978. Marxism as a Foundation for Urban Sociology. *Comparative Urban Research*, 4 (2, 3): 76-85.

Berman, Marshall. 1988. *All That is Solid Melts into Air: The Experience of Modernity.* New York: Penguin Books.

Castells, Manuel. 1976. Theory and Ideology in Urban Sociology. In *Urban Sociology: Critical Essays*, ed. Chris G. Pickvance: 60-84. London: Travistock Publishers. (Orig. 1969)

_____. 1977. *The Urban Question: A Marxist Approach.* London: Edward Arnold Publishers. (Orig. 1977 in French under the title of *La Question Urbaine*)

_____. 1992. The Space of Flows: Elements for a Theory of the New Urbanism in the Informational Society. Keynote paper at the Princeton University Conference on the New Urbanism, November.

_____. 1993. The Informational Economy and the New International Division of Labor. In *The New Global Economy in the Information Age: Reflections on Our Changing World*, eds. Martin Carnoy, et al.: 15-43. University Park: The Pennsylvania State University Press.

_____. 1996. *The Rise of the Network Society.* Oxford: Blackwell Publishers.

_____. 1998. *End of Millennium.* Oxford: Blackwell Publishers.

Castells, Manuel and Yuko Aoyama. 1994. Paths Towards the Informational Society: Employment Structure in G-7 Countries, 1920-1990. *International Labour Review*, 133 (1): 7-33.

CDC (Community Development Center). 1985. *Kawaba-mura to Setagaya-ku no Koryu ni tsuite* (The Exchange Program of Kawaba and Setagaya). Tokyo: CDC. (In Japanese)

Clavel, Pierre and William W. Goldsmith. 1973. Non-metropolitan Poverty and Community Institutions. *Community Development Society*, 4 (2): 76-93

Fischer, Claude S. 1978. On the Marxian Challenge to Urban Sociology. *Comparative Urban Research*, 4 (2, 3): 10-19.

_____. 1984. *The Urban Experience, 2nd ed*. San Diego, Harcourt Brace & Company.

Friedmann, John. 1992. *Empowerment: The Politics of Alternative Development*. Oxford: Blackwell Publishers.

Fujimoto, Isao. 1992. Lessons from Abroad in Rural Community Revitalization: The One Village, One Product Movement in Japan. *Community Development Journal*, 27 (1): 10-20.

Fuller, Anthony M. 1984. Part-Time Farming: The Enigmas and the Realities. In *Research in Rural Sociology and Development, Vol. 1, Focus on Agriculture*, ed. H. K. Schwarzweler: 187-219. Greenwich: Jai Press.

Goto, Junko. 1993. Rural Revitalization (Chiiki-okoshi) in Japan: A Case Study of Asuke Township. Ph.D. Dissertation, University of California, Los Angels.

Gottfried, Herbert. 1995. Corridor of Value: Rural Land in Rural Life. *Rural Development Perspectives*, 2 (1): 13-18.

Gunma-ken (Gunma Prefecture). 1997a. *Gunma no Jinko* (Statistical Outlook of Gunma's Population). Maebashi: Gunma Prefectural Government. (In Japanese)

_____. 1997b. *Shin-sangyo Koyo Soshutsu ni Kansuru Kenkyu Hokokusho* (Report on New Industries and Employment Generation). Maebashi: Gunma Prefectural Government. (In Japanese)

_____. 1999a. *Kenmin Techo* (Handbook for the People of Gunma Prefecture). Maebashi: Gunma Prefectural Government. (In Japanese)

_____. 1999b. *Gunma-ken Hoken Fukushi bu Kankei Shisetsu Ichiran* (List of Health/Welfare Facilities in Gunma). Maebashi: Gunma Prefectural Government. (In Japanese)

Harashobo. 1999. *Zenkoku Gakko Soran 2000* (List of Schools in Japan for the Year 2000). Tokyo: Harashobo. (In Japanese)

Harvey, David. 1978. On Countering the Marxian Myth: Chicago Style. *Comparative Urban Research*, 4 (2, 3): 28-45.

_____. 1985. *The Urbanization of Capitalism: Studies in the History and Theory of Capitalist Urbanization*. New York: St.Martin's Press.

_____. 1990. *The Conditions of Post-Modernity*. Oxford: Blackwell Publishers.

_____. 1994. Flexible Accumulation through Urbanization: Reflections on 'Post-modernism' in the American city. In *Post-Fordism: A*

Reader, ed. Ash Amin: 361-386. Oxford: Blackwell Publishers. (Orig. 1987 appeared in *Antipode,* 19 (3): 260-86)

_____. 1996. *Justice, Nature, and the Geography of Difference.* Oxford: Blackwell Publishers.

Hashiguchi, Takuya. 1996. Gunma-ken Kawaba-mura (Field Report on the Village of Kawaba, Gunma Prefecture). In *Chusankan Chiiki Kaihasu Seibi Kento Chosa* (Report on Rural Development in the Hilly and Mountainous Regions). Tokyo: Agricultural Policy Council: 209-215. (In Japanese)

Hasumi, Otohiko. 1968. Shihonshyugi no hattatsu to noson-shykai (Capitalist Development and Rural Societies). In *Noson Shyakai Gaku* (Rural Sociology), eds. Hiromich Yoda and Haruo Matsubara: 14-31. Tokyo: Kwashima Shyoten Publishers. (In Japanese)

Henderson, David M. 1997. Distance Doesn't Matter: Successful Tele-Business in the Highlands and Islands." Paper presented at Telebusiness International Conference in London, May 29.

Hettne, Bjorn. 1995. *Development Theory and the Three Worlds, 2nd. ed.* Essex: Longman Science & Technical.

Hill, Richard Child and Kuniko Fujita. 1995. Osaka's Tokyo Problem. *International Journal of Urban and Regional Research.* 19 (2): 181-193.

Hobshawn, Eric J. (ed). 1964. *Pre-capitalist Economic Formations.* London: Lawrence & Wishart.

Hoggart, Keith and Henry Buller. 1987. *Rural Development: A Geographical Perspective.* London: Routledge.

Kawaba-mura (Village of Kawaba). 1995. *Kawaba-mura Sogo Keikausho* (Comprehensive Development Plan of Kawaba). Kawaba: Kawaba Village Office. (In Japanese)

Kono, Naoya. 1994. Gunma-ken Kawaba-Mura to Tokyo-to Setagaya-ku no engumi ni tsuite (The Union of Kawaba, Gunma and Setagaya, Tokyo). *Kyodokumiai Keiei,* 490: 40-56. (In Japanese)

Kurabuchi-mura (Village of Kurabuchi). 1991. *Kurabuchi-mura Sogo Keikau* (Comprehensive Development Plan of Kurabuchi). Kurabuchi: Kurabuchi Village Ofice. (In Japanese)

_____. 1997. *Kurabuchimura Kleingarten no Gaiyo (The* Outline of the Kurabuchi Kleingarten). Pamphlet. Kurabuchi: Kurabuchi Village Ofice. (In Japanese)

Kurosawa, Takeo. 1985. *Kaso ni Idomu* (A Challenge against Decline). Tokyo: Seibun-sha. (In Japanese)

_____. 1996. *Michi wo Motomete: Yukoku no Nanatsu no Teigen* (Search for the Way: The Seven Patriotic Proposals). Tokyo: Oku Shuppan Service. (In Japanese)

Lefebvre, Henri. 1991. *The Production of Space.* Oxford: Blackwell Publishers. (Orig. 1974 in French under the title of *La Production de l'espace*)

Lobao, Linda. 1996. A Sociology of the Periphery Versus a Peripheral Sociology: Rural Sociology and the Dimension of Space. *Rural Sociology,* 61 (1): 77-102.

Mandel, Ernest. 1975. *Late Capitalism.* London: Verso. (Quoted in Soja 1989)

Markusen, Ann R. 1985. *Profit Cycles, Oligopoly, and Regional Development.* Cambridge: MIT Press.

Marsden, T. and J. Murdoch. 1991. Restructuring Rurality: Key Areas for Development in Assessing Rural Change. Working Paper 4: Countryside Change Initiative. University of Newcastle upon Tyne. (Quoted in Whatmore 1994)

Massey, Doreen. 1984. *Spatial Division of Labor: Social Structures and the Geography of Production.* New York, Routledge.

_____. 1993. Question of Locality. *Geography* 73 (2): 142-149.

MAFF (Minitry of Agriculture, Forestry and Fisheries). 1985 and 1995. *Census of Agriculture.* Tokyo: MAFF.

MITI (Ministry of International Trade and Industries), Research and Statistics Department. 1985 and 1995. *Census of Manufactures: Report by Cities, Towns and Villages.* Tokyo: MITI.

MITI (Ministry of International Trade and Industries) and Andersen Consulting. 1999. *Koyosakugen Sukekei Kekka: Kozotenkan Mekanizumu no Koshiku wo Mezashite* (Estimation Results: Towards Development of the Mechanism of Employment Restructuring). A Joint Report of MITI and Andersen. (In Japanese)

MPT (Ministry of Post and Telecommunications). 1997 and 1999. *Tsushin Hakusho (White Paper on Telecommunications).* Tokyo, Japan: Ookurasho Insakukyoku. (In Japanese)

Miyamoto, Kenichi. 1989. Kokusaika Jidai to Chiiki Seisaku (The Global Age and Regional Policies). In *Chiiki Keizai Gaku* (Regional Political Economy). eds. Kenicihi Miyamoto, et al.: 351-369. Tokyo: Yuhikaku. (In Japanese)

_____. 1990. *Kankyo keizaigaku* (Environmental Political Economy). Tokyo: Iwanami Shoten. (In Japanese)

_____. 1993. Japan's World Cities: Osaka and Tokyo Compared. In *Japanese Cities in the Global Economy*, eds. Kuniko Fujita and Richard Child Hill: 53-82. Philadelphia : Temple University Press.

Mizoo, Yoshitaka. 1994. *Kanko wo yomu* (A Tourism Reader). Tokyo: Kokon Shoin. (In Japanese)

_____. 1996. Gunmaken Niiharumura ni Okeru Rizoto Kaiahtsukeikaku to Rizoto Chiiki no Keiseikatei (The Planning of Resort Development and Establishment of Resort Areas in Niiharu-mura, Gunma Prefecture). *Annals of the Japan Association of Economic Geographers*. 42 (3):18-32. (In Japanese)

Mizuoka, Fujio. 1992. *Keizai chirigaku* (Economic Geography). Tokyo: Aoki Shoten. (In Japanese)

Moritomo, Yuichi. 1991. *Naihatuteki Hatten heno Michi* (The Road towards Endogenous Development). Tokyo: Nosangyoson Bunka Kyokai. (In Japanese)

Nakajima, Naoko. 1992. Gunma-ken Kawaba-mura ni Okeru Noringyo to Kankoka (Recent Development of Tourism and Past and Present Agroforestry in Kawaba-mura, Gunma Prefecture). *Annals of Ochanomizu Geographical Society*, 33: 45-56. (In Japanese)

Nerfin, M. (ed.). 1997. *Another Development: Approaches and Strategies*. Uppsala: The Dag Hammarskjöld Foundation. (Quoted in Hette 1995)

Niiharu-mura (Village of Niiharu). 1996. *Niiharu-mura Daisanji Sogokeikaku* (The Third Comprehensive Development Plan of Niiharu). Niiharu: Niiharu Village Office.

Nobunkyo (Rural Culture Association). 1994. Daishosoho no Sangyo Okoshi: Gunma Sawada Nokyono Jissen (The Practices of Sawada Agricultural Cooperative). *Shizen to Ningen wo Musubu*, July 1994. (In Japanese)

Osti, Giorgio. 1997. Sustainable Development in the Italian Mountains. In *Sustainable Rural Development*, eds. Henk de Haan, et al.: 179-198. Aldershot: Ashgate Publishing.

Ouchi, Tsutomu. 1963. *Nihon-Keizai-Ron, Vol. II* (A Study on Japanese Economy, Vol. II). Tokyo: University of Tokyo Press. (In Japanese)

Pahl, R. E. 1996. The Rural-Urban Continuum. *Sociologia Ruralis*, 6: 299-329.

Piore, Michael J. and Charles F. Sabel. 1984. *The Second Industrial Divide: Possibilities for Prosperity*. New York: Basic Books.

Prime Minister's Office, Japan. 1987. *Nihonjin no Shokuseikatu to Shokuryo Mondai (Opinion Polls on Diet and Food Issues in Japan)*. Tokyo:

Sorifu Kohoshitsu (Division of Public Relations, Prime Minister's Office, Japan).

Relph, Edward. 1993. Modernity and the Reclamation of Place. In *Dwelling Seeing and Designing, Toward a Phenomenological Ecology*, ed. David Seamon: 25-40. Albany: SUNY Press.

SAC (Sawada Agricultural Cooperative). 1997. *Mura-zukuri to Sangyo-Okoshi Heno Chosen* (The Challenge for Village Building and Industrial Development: Sixth Five-Year Plan). Nakanojo: SAC. (In Japanese)

Sachs, Wolfgang. 1992. One World. In *The Development Dictionary: A Guide to Knowledge as Power*, ed. Wolfgang Sachs: 102-115. London: Zed Books.

Schumpeter, Joseph A. 1983. *The Theory of Economic Development: An Inquiry into Profits, Capital, Credit, Interest, and the Business Cycle*. New Brunswick: Transaction Books. (Orig. 1912)

_____. 1994. *Capitalism, Socialism and Democracy*. London: Routledge. (Orig. 1942)

Smith, Adam. 1937. *An Inquiry into the Nature and Causes of the Wealth of Nations*. New York: Modern Library. (Orig. 1776)

Soja, Edward W. 1989. *Postmodern Geographies: The Reassertion of Space in Critical Social Theory*. London: Verso.

Sorokin, Pitirim and Carle C. Zimmerman. 1929. *Principles of Rural-Urban Sociology*. New York: Henry Holt and Company.

Soros, George. 1998. *The Crisis of Global Capitalism: Open Society Endangered*. New York: Public Affairs.

Statistical Information Institute for Consulting and Analysis (Tokeijoho kenkyu kaiatsu center). 1997. *Shikuchson betsu shorai suikei jinko (Projected Population by Municipalities)*. Tokyo: SIICA. (Diskettes containing statistical data)

Statistics Office, Management and Coordination Agency. 1985 and 1995. *Population Census of Japan*. Tokyo: Management and Coordination Agency.

Sugiura, Yoichi and John K. Gillrspie. 1994. *Nihon Bunka wo Eigo de Shokai Suru Jiten (Traditional Japanese Culture and Modern Japan)*. Tokyo: Natume Sha. (Written bilingually in Japanese and English)

Suzuki, Kazuo. 1998. *Noson no Shimei, Sosite Chosen (The Role of Rural Villages, and our Challenge)*. Pamphlet. Niiharu: Niiharu Village Office. (In Japanese)

Takahashi, Masao. 1985. Fukugoteki na Mura-Zukukuri (Multiple Strategies of Village Development: The Case of SAC). In *Mura no chosen* (The Challenge of Villages), eds. Masao Takahashi: 130-151. Tokyo: Ienohikari. (In Japanse)

Takahashi, Yoshio. 1986. *Inaka Gurashi no Kofuku* (Happiness from Living in the Countryside). Tokyo: Soshi Sha. (In Japanese)

Takahashi, Yuetsu. 1988. Chiiki Shakai (Regional Societies). In *Shakaigaku-gairon* (Introductory Sociology), eds. Kohei Honma et al.: 293-318. Tokyo: Yuhikaku Publishers. (In Japanese)

Kiyonari, Tadao. 1986. *Chiiki Sangyo Seisaku* (Regional Industrial Policy). Tokyo: University of Tokyo Press. (In Japanese; Quoted in Goto 1993).

Tökei, Ferenc. 1977. *Shakai Koseitai Ron*. Tokyo: Miraisha Publishers. (In Japanese; Orig. 1968 in Hungarian under the title *Á Tarsadalmi Formák Elméletéhez*)

_____. 1979. *Essays on the Asiatic Mode of Production*. Budapest: Akadémiai Kiadó.

_____. 1989. Introduction. In *Primitive Society and Asiatic Mode of Production*, ed. Ferenc Tökei: 7-32. Budapest: MTA Orientalisztikai Munkaközösséc.

Tönnies, Ferdinand. 1963. *Community and Society*. New York: Harper and Row. (Orig. 1887 in German under the title *Gemeinschaft und Geselltschaft*)

Vietorisz, Thomas. 1991. The Global Information Economy, Privatization, and the Future of Socialism. Paper presented at Socialist Conference, Budapest

Vietorisz, Thomas and Alan McAdams. 1995. *Paradigms for Industrial Development as Applied to Mexico*. Unpublished paper for PEMIX, Cornell University.

Watanabe, Takasuke. 1984. Setagaya Kumin Mura no Kihon Keikaku (Basic Plan of Setagaya's Kenko-mura). In *Doboku Kogaku Taikei 30 (Civil Engineering Series, Vol. 30)*, eds. Tadayoshi Suzuki: 264-278. Tokyo: Shokoku Sha. (In Japanese)

Weber, Max. 1958. *The City*. Glencoe: Free Press.

Whatmore, Sarah. 1994. Global Agro-Food Complexes and the Refashioning of Rural Europe. In *Globalization, Institutions, and Regional Development in Europe*, eds. Ash Amin and Nigel Thrift: 46-67. Oxford: Oxford University Press.

Wiggin, Geoffrey W. 1985. Rural/Urban Exchange Programs. In *Noson no Kyoryu ni Yoru Nogyo Noson no Shinko ni Kansuru Chosa Hoku Sho (A report on Rural Promotion through Rural/Urban Exchanges)*, eds. Takeo Ogawa et al.:251-254. Tokyo: Agricultural Policy Research Council.

Wirth, Louis. 1938. Urbanism as a Way of Life. *American Journal of Sociology*. 44 (July): 33-24.